THE LITTLE BOOK OF
Environment
and
Restorative Justice

THE LITTLE BOOKS OF JUSTICE & PEACEBUILDING

Published titles include:

The Little Book of Restorative Justice: Revised & Updated, by Howard Zehr

The Little Book of Conflict Transformation, by John Paul Lederach

The Little Book of Family Group Conferences, New-Zealand Style,
by Allan MacRae and Howard Zehr

The Little Book of Strategic Peacebuilding, by Lisa Schirch

The Little Book of Strategic Negotiation, by Jayne Seminare Docherty

The Little Book of Circle Processes, by Kay Pranis

The Little Book of Contemplative Photography, by Howard Zehr

Little Book of Healthy Organizations, by David Brubaker and Ruth Hoover Zimmerman

The Little Book of Restorative Discipline for Schools, by Lorraine Stutzman Amstutz
and Judy H. Mullet

The Little Book of Trauma Healing, by Carolyn Yoder

The Little Book of Biblical Justice, by Chris Marshall

The Little Book of Restorative Justice for People in Prison, by Barb Toews

The Little Book of Cool Tools for Hot Topics, by Ron Kraybill and Evelyn Wright

El Pequeño Libro de Justicia Restaurativa, by Howard Zehr

The Little Book of Dialogue for Difficult Subjects, by Lisa Schirch and David Campt

The Little Book of Victim Offender Conferencing, by Lorraine Stutzman Amstutz

The Little Book of Restorative Justice for Colleges and Universities, by David R. Karp

The Little Book of Restorative Justice for Sexual Abuse, by Judah Oudshoorn
with Michelle Jackett and Lorraine Stutzman Amstutz

The Big Book of Restorative Justice: Four Classic Justice & Peacebuilding Books in One Volume,
by Howard Zehr, Lorraine Stutzman Amstutz, Allan MacRae, and Kay Pranis

The Little Book of Transformative Community Conferencing, by David Anderson Hooker

The Little Book of Restorative Justice in Education, by Katherine Evans
and Dorothy Vaandering

The Little Book of Restorative Justice for Older Adults, by Julie Friesen and Wendy Meek

The Little Book of Race and Restorative Justice, by Fania E. Davis

The Little Book of Racial Healing, by Thomas Norman DeWolf, Jodie Geddes

The Little Book of Restorative Teaching Tools,
by Lindsey Pointer, Kathleen McGoey, and Haley Farrar

Little Book of Restorative Teaching Tools for Online Learning,
by Kathleen McGoey and Lindsey Pointer

The Little Book of Police Youth Dialogue, by Dr. Micah E. Johnson and Jeffrey Weisberg

The Little Book of Youth Engagement in Restorative Justice, by Evelín Aquino,
Heather Bligh Manchester, and Anita Wadhwa

The Little Book of Restorative Justice Program Design, by Alisa Del Tufo and E. Quin Gonell

Little Book of Listening, by Sharon Browning, Donna Duffey, Fred Magondu,
John A. Moore, and Patricia A. Way

Little Book of Restorative Justice for Campus Sexual Harms,
by Rachel Roth Sawatzky and Mikayla W-C McCray

The Little Books of Justice & Peacebuilding present, in highly accessible form, key concepts and practices from the fields of restorative justice, conflict transformation, and peacebuilding. Written by leaders in these fields, they are designed for practitioners, students, and anyone interested in justice, peace, and conflict resolution.

The Little Books of Justice & Peacebuilding series is a cooperative effort between the Center for Justice and Peacebuilding of Eastern Mennonite University and publisher Good Books.

THE LITTLE BOOK OF
Environment and Restorative Justice

A Multidimensional Approach to Undoing Settler Harms

Waŋbli Wapȟáha Hokšíla,
Nirson Medeiros da Silva Neto,
João Salm, and
Josineide Gadelha Pamplona Medeiros

New York, New York

Copyright © 2025 by Waŋblí Wapȟáha Hokšíla, Nirson Medeiros da Silva Neto, João Salm, and Josineide Gadelha Pamplona Medeiros

All rights reserved. No part of this book may be reproduced in any manner without the express written consent of the publisher, except in the case of brief excerpts in critical reviews or articles. All inquiries should be addressed to Good Books, 307 West 36th Street, 11th Floor, New York, NY 10018.

Good Books books may be purchased in bulk at special discounts for sales promotion, corporate gifts, fund-raising, or educational purposes. Special editions can also be created to specifications. For details, contact the Special Sales Department, Good Books, 307 West 36th Street, 11th Floor, New York, NY 10018 or info@skyhorsepublishing.com.

Good Books is an imprint of Skyhorse Publishing, Inc.®, a Delaware corporation.

Visit our website at www.goodbooks.com.

10 9 8 7 6 5 4 3 2 1

Library of Congress Cataloging-in-Publication Data is available on file.

Cover design by Kai Texel
Cover photo by Howard Zehr
Series editor: Barb Toews

Print ISBN: 978-1-68099-963-1
Ebook ISBN: 978-1-68099-972-3

Printed in the United States of America

Contents

Indigenous Land Acknowledgments — vii

Chapter 1: Environment and Restorative Justice:
An Overview — 1
Settler Colonialism and Environmental Crisis — 3
Being Good Relatives — 4
Restorative Justice and Multidimensionality — 6
About This Book — 7

Chapter 2: Settler Colonialism and the Environment — 10
The First Harm — 11
Settler Environmentalism — 13
Postponing the End of the World — 22

Chapter 3: Environmental Justice and
Environmental Racism — 24
The First Step: Memphis Sanitation Strikes — 25
Environmental Justice and Racism — 26
Principles of Environmental Justice — 28
Mní Wičhóni Movement: An Indigenous
Perspective on Environmental Justice — 31
Standing with the Environment Together — 34

Chapter 4: Restoring the Broken Kinship — 36
Wildfires in California: Settler Colonialism and
Disruption of TEK — 37
"Good Fires": Partnering with Fire Kin — 39

"The Environment" Is People	42
We Are All Relatives	46
The Good Living: An Indigenous Ethic	46

Chapter 5: Making Strangers Relatives — 49
- "This Is the Justice We Want" — 50
- Restorative Justice and Circles — 54
- Making Strangers into Relatives — 59
- It's About Love — 63

Chapter 6: Multidimensional Restorative Justice — 66
- Guarani Kaiowa's Land Reclamation — 67
- A Multidimensional Restorative Justice Framework — 71
- Multifocal Lens — 86
- A Compass, Not a Map — 90

Chapter 7: The Eagle and the Condor — 92

Resources — 97
Acknowledgments — 101
About the Authors — 104
Notes — 106

Indigenous Land Acknowledgments

Greetings from my homeland, the Očhéthi Šakówiŋ Oyáte Makȟóčhe (People of the Seven Council Fires territory). Our homeland is where our relatives come from, where our relatives live, and where our relatives love and defend each other. To coexist with our relatives is a difficult responsibility but one made more so ever since settlers invaded our homeland. Settlers, among other things, have nearly exterminated our relative the Tȟatȟáŋka Oyáte (Buffalo Nation). Compared to 150 years ago, few of them survive today. Settlers have enclosed our relative the Mní Oyáte (Water Nation). There are several structures built on the Mní Šoše (a.k.a. the Missouri River) that, like bondage, constrain the Mní Oyáte's natural, life-giving flow. Settlers have drilled into our relative, Uŋčí Makȟá (Grandmother Earth). The drilling has left our Grandmother Earth with notable scars: Mount Rushmore, Crazy Horse Monument, Homestake Mine, the Dakota Access Pipeline, and abandoned radiation testing sites. Settlers have illegally colonized and, therefore, unlawfully reside in our homeland. We have never consented to these and other colonizer-led harms. Hence, the litmus test of any land acknowledgment is the rightful return of stolen Native land.

—Waŋblí Wapȟáha Hokšíla (Edward Valandra)

Next to the entrance of the Chicago Cultural Center, we can read that, according to the American Indian Center of Chicago, the city where I live "is the traditional homelands of the Council of the Three Fires: the Odawa, Ojibwe and Potawatomi Nations. Many other Tribes like the Miami, Ho-Chunk, Sac and Fox also called this area home. American Indians continue to call this area home and now Chicago is home to the third largest Urban American Indian community that still practices their heritage, traditions and care for the land and waterways. Today, Chicago continues to be a place that calls many people from diverse backgrounds to live and gather here."

—João Salm

A large part of this little book was written in Belém and Santarém, Brazilian Amazon cities, which are respectively the original homelands of the Tupinambá and Tapajó Peoples. These two Amazonian cities are today the home of many other Indigenous Peoples who live in urban and rural areas. Despite the settlers' attempts to eliminate and displace them, Amazonian Native Peoples are still here. They are alive and resist. Indigenous Peoples are not groups who remained in the past. They are our relatives with whom

we share our existence contemporaneously and deserve respect like any other People. We recognize that, in the Amazon region, all lands were originally Indigenous lands and many of them continue to be Indigenous territories which need to be respected and protected today.
—Josineide Pamplona e Nirson Neto

Chapter 1
Environment and Restorative Justice: An Overview

We begin this little book by sharing two interconnected stories from Brazil, although the link between them does not seem evident at first glance.

In 2024, one of the greatest climate tragedies in South America occurred in Rio Grande do Sul, a Brazilian state primarily inhabited by descendants of European settlers. An unprecedented increase in rainfall over several weeks has led to the flooding of rivers and the inundation of entire cities, claiming nearly two hundreds lives and destroying homes, vehicles, public buildings, crops, and roads. This climate event resulted in a lack of drinking water, the spread of diseases, and the displacement of thousands of families. The natural disaster in Rio Grande do Sul left countless people in extreme vulnerability. They were taken to shelters, where they remained until they could return to their homes, if those homes were not destroyed. Furthermore, the damage caused by the flooding dramatically impacted many domestic and farm animals, resulting in a horrifying zoological emergency.

A few years ago, another crisis arose involving the Yanomami, an Indigenous People residing in an environmentally conserved area of the Amazon rainforest. Miners, who came from various regions of Brazil, invaded the Yanomami's homeland. Similar to settler invasions elsewhere, this incursion brought devastating epidemics to their lands, resulting in the deaths of hundreds of Yanomami community members. Previous intrusions had already inflicted harm and even the extermination of neighboring Indigenous Peoples. In addition to diseases, the illegal occupation of Yanomami land led to murders and violent conflicts between Indigenous Peoples and the invaders, rivers became muddy and contaminated with mercury, the forest was cleared in some areas, and animals were driven or frightened away from their natural habitats. This contemporary settler assault on the environment has led to a health crisis and starvation for Indigenous communities, particularly impacting children and the elderly.

To many people, these two events—the flooding and the invasion—may seem unrelated and have nothing to do with each other. The flood, being a natural occurrence, appears to lack or have no direct culprits. However, we cannot deny that the flooding was a natural disaster driven by climate change, which is happening globally, along with human behaviors that have contributed to this change. The settler invasion has more easily identifiable perpetrators. There are both direct and indirect responsibilities, including those related to the state and businesses, for systematic violations of Indigenous Peoples' rights, not just those of the Yanomami.

But these tragic events are deeply interconnected. We argue here in this little book that climate catastrophes are connected to settler colonialism.[1] Settler colonialism is a form of colonization where settlers, typically from foreign countries and cultures, migrate to new territories with the goal of permanently settling and asserting control over them. This logic inherently uses strategies such as forced displacement, genocide, and ethnic cleansing to achieve settler goals: occupy and lastingly remain on stolen land. To do so often causes environmental harm, leading to severe damage to the Natural World. This colonialism is not just a mere past event; rather, it is an ongoing structure that continues to shape the present.

How shall we address the environmental injustices and damages resulting from settler colonialism? Drawing inspiration from Indigenous Peoples, we contend that the restoration of kinship, the embrace of relationality, and a nuanced understanding of addressing the complexities of environmental harm and injustice is the answer. It may sound unusual, but allow us to elaborate further.

Settler Colonialism and Environmental Crisis

You have likely studied in school, read books, visited museums, watched TV, listened to podcasts, or researched websites about the diverse human groups that inhabited the Americas before the arrival of European settlers. Perhaps you've heard that many ecosystems in both North and South America are examples of "domesticated nature"—areas that have been "exploited" and "controlled" by humans since time immemorial. You may also know that Indigenous

Peoples have never transformed their environments in a destructive way. Thus, you understand that "your lands" were already inhabited long before the arrival of European settlers or others from different regions and their descendants, and the environmental harm in such lands was a direct result of the behavior and lifestyle of foreign people (from this point forward, "settlers" will refer to this group of people).

Contrary to the typical settlers' narrative, these lands were neither empty nor unproductive before their arrival. They were home to many Indigenous Peoples who lived and continue to live there. These communities maintain a balance with the Natural World, just as their ancestors did, and have never mistreated or degraded "it" as settlers have done and continue to do. Settler occupation severely disrupted that balanced relationship with other-than-human beings. In this book, "other-than-human beings" refers to all living things beyond humans, including animals, plants, waters, rocks, air, fire, hills, mountains, thunder, the sun, the moon, and even spiritual or nonmaterial forces.

To address current environmental catastrophes, we must learn from Indigenous Peoples. Their traditional ecological knowledge offers insights on how humans can live connected to the Natural World and restore balance where it has been disrupted.

Being Good Relatives

Indigenous Peoples from Abya Yala—a term for what settlers eventually renamed the "American" continents—focus on the concept of "good living" in their homelands. "Good living"—also referred to as "good life" or "good conviviality"—is an English translation of Indigenous terms that express the relationship between humans and all living beings. While settlers concern themselves with "the environment," Native Peoples prioritize relationality and coexisting with all living beings in a balanced way. They do not view the Natural World as a detached "it" or "thing" but rather as an engaged, subjective "you" or "us," inseparable from humanity. For them, all beings that make up the Natural World possess personality and deserve our utmost care, respect, and consideration—if not rights. Consequently, you'll notice that we capitalize words for other-than-human beings, such as Fire and Water.

The Očhéthi Šakówiŋ Oyáte (People of the Seven Fire Council, also known as Lakȟóta, Dakȟóta, and Nakȟóta, or the Sioux Nation) recognize that all beings—humans and other living entities—share the same energy force from a Creator. They express this with the phrase Mitákuye Oyás'iŋ (All My Relatives). As a result, they emphasize the importance of being good relatives to one another.

While this viewpoint is Indigenous, it is not entirely unfamiliar to Western thought. For instance, settler cultures deeply influenced by Christian beliefs refer to themselves as God's children, and in that spirit of fellowship, they address each other as brothers and sisters. Saint Francis of Assisi even spoke of Brother Sun and Sister Moon, referring to these other-than-human beings. Because of this, kindness is expected in their interactions. Thus, through fellowship, settlers create a different form of kinship that transcends genetic or blood ties, somewhat resembling, but not exactly like, the kinship found in Indigenous cultures.

This finding encourages both Indigenous Peoples and settlers to establish proper relations with all our relatives. From this perspective, the environment is as worthy as humankind, and vice versa. We have a moral responsibility to build and sustain a beloved community with all living beings, including nonhumans, and not to harm them as good relatives would. Teachings from peoples who have inhabited these lands since time immemorial (which we now call home) inspire us to be good relatives to the Natural World.

Restorative Justice and Multidimensionality

We believe that restorative justice theory and practices might offer a pathway to being good relatives. As a global movement and social philosophy, restorative justice is a way of imagining, practicing, and living justice[2] in a way that requires us to be responsible in our relationships with each other and ourselves. It requires us to recognize the harm we have caused and be aware of how we can actively take responsibility for it. This approach involves those who inflict harm—including governments and corporations, in some instances—and those who experience the harm in processes aimed at repairing wrongs, preventing the recurrence of harmful behaviors, and transforming the underlying structures and narratives that perpetuate harm.

For decades, restorative justice efforts have focused on addressing harms related to interpersonal relationships (e.g., within the criminal justice system) and the community. More recently, the vision and practice of restorative justice have broadened to confront harm-doing and violence at the societal level, including structural and systemic violence, historical traumas and their consequences, and intergenerational harms. This expanded understanding of restorative justice encompasses environmental harm and injustice, which seriously affects both the Natural World and human beings. However, few restorative justice practitioners and scholars engage with the legacy and aftermath of settler colonialism, and even fewer have explored its connection to the environmental crisis we are currently experiencing.

In Abya Yala, ecological debates cannot be divorced from settler colonialism. To tackle these complex issues, we suggest restorative justice adopt a multidimensional framework. This framework transcends the economic concerns that frequently dominate settler discussions on environmental mitigation. Instead, it considers the psychological, relational, social, economic, political, cultural, ecological, and spiritual dimensions of life, offering a holistic perspective of justice, deeply inspired by Indigenous Peoples. Throughout this book, we will delve deeper into this idea and its implications for addressing environmental harm and injustice.

About This Book

This little book invites us to think collectively about addressing the environmental issues plaguing our world—one that repairs the harms of settler colonialism and calls us to be good relatives to the Natural World. To tackle systemic environmental problems, the following pages offer much more than a call to exercise our imagination; they also present an urgent call to action to apply the concepts, principles, values, and methodologies associated with restorative justice. Given the contexts from which the authors originate, the focus is primarily on two settler states: the

United States and Brazil. However, we contend that the words and reflections are valuable and adaptable to other regions of the world.

The approach presented in the following pages draws inspiration from various sources, including the Očhéthi Šakówiŋ Oyaté's worldview, the Brazilian socio-environmental movement, the struggles for environmental justice in the United States, and the idea of multidimensionality in the work of African Brazilian sociologist Alberto Guerreiro Ramos. This knowledge is complemented by the coauthors' theoretical and practical experiences as Indigenous peoples and settlers in restorative justice. Consequently, this book represents a dialogue between Lakota (Waŋblí Wapȟáha Hokšíla) and settler (João Salm, Nirson Neto, and Josineide Pamplona) authors from Northern and Southern Abya Yala. It is akin to a joint flight of the Eagle and the Condor, as the ancient Indigenous prophecy suggested. We speak about this prophecy in the closing chapter.

Before reading the next chapter, we recommend that you go to the end of the book to read the "About the Authors" section, where we introduce ourselves. Knowing who we are and where we come from is an Indigenous protocol and necessary first step for treating each other as relatives. If you haven't already, we also suggest reading the "Indigenous Land Acknowledgments" that precede this chapter, as they discuss the Indigenous homelands from which we wrote this book, many of which were stolen or significantly impacted by settlers.

The rest of the book takes you on a journey to understand the connections among settler colonialism, Indigenous Peoples' relationship with the

Natural World, and pathways to repair the harm that has been done and continues to be done to the environment. Chapter 2 discusses how settler colonialism has led to environmental damage in Abya Yala and outlines the various waves of environmentalism that settlers have used to mitigate these harms, which is primarily rooted in an anthropocentric worldview. Chapter 3 shifts focus to the environmental justice movement in the United States, which brings a broader perspective to environmental debates by confronting racism and the unequal distribution of environmental damage and risks. Chapter 4 then transitions to explore the Indigenous view that all living beings, including other-than-humans, are people and relatives and what this understanding signifies for the protection of the Natural World.

Drawing from the Oyáte's perspective of transforming strangers into relatives and the practice of peacemaking circles, Chapter 5 presents restorative justice. In Chapter 6, this understanding expands into a multidimensional approach to restorative justice that seeks to heal the harm caused to both the Natural World and Indigenous Peoples by settler colonialism. Finally, in Chapter 7, we conclude by using a metaphor to illustrate how settlers and Indigenous Peoples can come together to heal environmental wounds.

We wish you a good journey!

Chapter 2
Settler Colonialism and the Environment

Environmentalism without class struggle is gardening.
—Chico Mendes

Settler colonialism began in Abya Yala, the American continents, more than five hundred years ago. Since then, European settlers and their descendants (herein referred to as "settlers") have wrongly viewed Indigenous Peoples' homelands as empty and unproductive spaces. Even today, settlers propagate a narrative that they alone "discovered" a world that has been inhabited for millennia by millions of Native peoples, consisting of thousands of national groups with distinct names, cultures, and languages. This settler perspective purports that these areas must be occupied and developed, regardless of Indigenous Peoples' views concerning their lands and ways of living in them. This chapter examines this settler viewpoint through the history of colonization and genocide, beginning with the First Harm and its impact on settlers' relationships with the environment. We then outline three waves of environmentalism, each developed with the intention of mitigating settler harms.

The First Harm

The "Doctrine of Discovery" has been taught for centuries without question until recently. This doctrine consists of a set of fictional legal principles that European nations fabricated to justify their rights to claim and rule over "new lands." These principles asserted that Europeans could lay claim to lands inhabited by people they deemed "uncivilized," "primitive," "savage," often merely because they were not Christians. Settlers have used, and continue to use, this doctrine to justify the theft of Indigenous lands they invaded. Much damage has occurred since settlers adopted this doctrine in Abya Yala and many other places worldwide.

The theft of Indigenous lands is marked as what is now referred to as the First Harm. It resulted in the genocide of countless Native Peoples, a narrative that settlers rarely acknowledge or share, and caused environmental damage, or what we call ecocide, including deforestation, water contamination, land poisoning, biodiversity loss, and air pollution. In the US context, two instances of ecocide are the settlers' indiscriminate slaughter of Thatȟáŋka Oyáte (Buffalo People) and the destruction of Tȟuŋkášila Šákpe (the Six Grandfathers) due to the creation of Mount Rushmore.

Thatȟáŋka Oyáte (Buffalo People)

In the mid-nineteenth century, as American settlers invaded the Great Plains, they sought to close a frontier that separated the eastern and western United

States. This invasion coincided with a growing market for buffalo hides, resulting in the slaughter of tens of millions of buffalo. Beyond their motivations lay the reality that the Očhéthi Šakówiŋ Oyáte (hereafter referred to as Oyáte), who lived in the Great Plains, had a long-standing relationship with the Tȟatȟáŋka Oyáte (the Buffalo People or Nation), which served as a primary source of livelihood for many Native Peoples from Abya Yala North (Turtle Island or North America). By cleansing the Tȟatȟáŋka Oyáte from the Great Plains, settlers could also eradicate Indigenous Peoples who resisted the invasion of their homelands. The settlers' actions of ecocide and genocide led to the near extinction of both the Buffalo Nation and the Očhéthi Šakówiŋ Oyáte.

Tȟuŋkášila Šákpe (Six Grandfathers)

In the early twentieth century, American settlers built the infamous Mount Rushmore in Pahá Sápa (Black Hills), the Oyáte's unceded territory, without obtaining their consent. The US landmark was carved into a sacred space of the Oyáte, Tȟuŋkášila Šákpe (the Six Grandfathers). Each of the Six Grandfathers represents one of the six spiritual directions: West, North, East, South, Above (Sky), and Below (Earth). For many Indigenous Peoples, Mount Rushmore constitutes outrageous settler arrogance because the four white US presidents (George Washington, Thomas Jefferson, Abraham Lincoln, and Theodore Roosevelt) depicted on the monument represent Native-hating. The settlers' behavior toward the Natural World and their violation of the 1868 Treaty of Fort Laramie—in which the settlers recognized the Oyáte's exclusive and undisturbed use of the Black Hills in perpetuity—left irreparable wounds on both Uŋčí Makȟá (Grandmother Earth) and the Oyáte's national soul. What the settlers did is regarded as an unforgivable act.

Settler Environmentalism

Settler colonialism caused severe damage to the Natural World, exemplified by Tȟatȟáŋka Oyáte and Tȟuŋkášila Šákpe. These and other environmental harms raised awareness in settler societies about the need for ecological conservation to protect endangered ecosystems and other-than-human species. Over time, they also recognized the necessity of developing society in ways that are less harmful to Nature. The following section outlines the primary strategies settlers have employed to mitigate environmental destruction, which we refer to as settler environmentalism.

Environmental Reservations

For decades, environmental reservations have been the primary strategy for conservation among settlers. You have likely already visited one—such as nature preserves, parks, wildlife refuges, wetlands, or national heritage lands. Yellowstone National Park, located in Wyoming, Montana, and Idaho, stands as the iconic symbol of this strategy and is a source of great pride for American settlers. Established in 1872, it was the first settler-designated environmental reservation in Abya Yala North. While it started a movement that spread throughout the United States and the world, it was not the first environmental reservation. On one hand, before there was an "American" identity, the United Kingdom's royal family already designated protected forests for their exclusive use. On the other hand, settlers themselves established Indian reservations for Indigenous Peoples in order to open their "non-reservation" territory for white homesteading. Although this latter reservation was not intended for environmental conservation, it unintentionally guaranteed spaces for Nature's protection.

The environmental reservation model is closely linked to the Romanticism movement. During the nineteenth century, art and literature approached Nature from a contemplative perspective. The underlying concept of environmental reservations is to conserve designated parts of the Natural World in their primitive state, just as they were before the settlers' arrival. More than merely a strategy for protecting natural spaces, the model embodies a philosophy that separates us from Nature. It aims to shield these areas from harmful human intervention by establishing protected spaces. These areas are where people supposedly refresh themselves, recover from life's stresses, or revere Nature. Antonio Carlos Diegues, a Brazilian professor who studied this model, once stated that environmental reservations represent a rational and modern interpretation of the myth of "paradise lost"—a place that humans (namely, the settlers) long for after their ancestors' expulsion from biblical Eden.[1]

Although environmental reservations have become an essential model of environmental conservation, very few settlers acknowledge, or have been socialized to forget, that this model was built at the expense of Indigenous Peoples. Almost all the environmentally conserved areas in Abya Yala, both in the North and South, are lands where Native Peoples lived long before the arrival of settlers. Indeed, many Indigenous Peoples suffered loss so that environmental reserves could be established. Yosemite National Park and Great Smoky Mountains National Park are two notable examples.

Yosemite National Park

An early example of harm concerns the popular and celebrated Yosemite National Park in California, which played a pivotal role in the development of the environmental reservation concept. In 1851, the Mariposa Battalion, a militia composed of white miners, was formed. Without justification, they hunted down and killed with impunity Miwok People. The Miwoks' only "crime" was being Native people living in the area. This horrific genocide of the Miwok paved the way for the 1890 creation of Yosemite National Park, which was carved out of their ancestral homeland. Following the genocide, efforts to protect Yosemite Valley led to President Abraham Lincoln's signing of the Yosemite Grant in 1864, which designated the area as federally protected land, laying the groundwork for the National Park System.[2]

Great Smoky Mountains National Park

The Great Smoky Mountains National Park, located in North Carolina and Tennessee, was chartered by the US Congress in 1934 and officially dedicated by President Franklin D. Roosevelt in 1940. It is a destination many American people enjoy visiting to feel close to Nature, whether watching bears, visiting waterfalls, or camping deep in the forest. Cherokee, a small Indigenous city located near the National Park, is an almost obligatory tourist destination for anyone exploring the Great Smoky Mountains. There, visitors love to observe Native ways of life and listen to stories of the first inhabitants. Perhaps they even fantasize about being "noble savages" or Pretendians (settlers who claim and appropriate Indigenous identities despite not belonging to Indigenous Peoples).

Despite admiring the lifestyles and stories of Native peoples, settler visitors can, and often do, avoid acknowledging the First Harm. Take the Eastern Band of Cherokee Indians. They are the descendants of Cherokees who resisted forced removal from their homelands in the Southeastern United States to Indian Territory (present-day Oklahoma). This forced removal is remembered among the Cherokee as the Trail of Tears, during which an estimated 25 percent of the Cherokees died along the way. Those who remained in the East had little choice but to assimilate, embrace Christianity, and learn English. When they reorganized as a tribe, they had to repurchase land that had been stolen from them by the United States. So, their current land, a small fragment of their original homeland, is not a typical reservation but rather a land trust supervised by the Bureau of Indian Affairs.

Eco-Efficiency

Due to the growing awareness of the shortcomings and settler violence associated with environmental reservations, a new strategy has gained popularity throughout the twentieth century: eco-efficiency. This scientifically inspired alternative model has become one of the leading fads of settler environmentalism, serving as a foundation for various discourses and methodologies related to environmental protection, including debates on sustainable development.

The eco-efficiency model posits that human groups' relationship with the environment is not grounded in reverence for the Natural World, a desire to protect it from human intervention, or an aesthetic and spiritual appreciation of wildlife.[3] Instead, it is based on the pursuit of maximum sustainable production "by reducing waste and inefficiency in the exploitation and consumption of non-renewable natural resources."[4] This model emphasizes the productive potential of the Natural World, aiming to achieve the greatest possible social, economic, and environmental benefits for both present and future generations.

Eco-efficiency lies at the heart of environmentally friendly practices including selective waste collection, biodegradable industrial products, solid waste reuse, biofuels, clean energy, and carbon reduction. It also guides our contemporary understanding of sustainable development, meaning that the needs of the present generation should be met without compromising future generations' ability to meet their own needs. This understanding of sustainability implies optimal harmonization between three elements: economic growth, social justice, and environmental conservation. The United Nations 2030 Agenda, which introduced the Sustainable Development Goals (SDGs), underscores peace as a fourth element, stating that "there can be no sustainable development without peace and no peace without sustainable development."[5]

On the surface, eco-efficiency seems like an excellent way to protect the environment. Undoubtedly, it presents a more complex, multidimensional model than its predecessor. However, upon critical analysis, eco-efficiency does not differ greatly from environmental reservations. It also suffers from an anthropocentric perspective. Conservation focuses more on human needs, interests, desires, and goals than on protecting the Natural World. Although concerned with social justice, environmental conservation, and peace, this approach is centered on development—defined as economic growth—which inevitably brings harm to both humans and nonhumans, particularly the most vulnerable and marginalized individuals and groups in settler societies. An example of this approach is seen in the Amazon rainforest, which is the homeland of numerous Indigenous Peoples, and the Brazil nut gatherers.

Brazil Nut Gatherers vs. Jari Project

Over fifty years ago, American businessman Daniel Keith Ludwig started the Jari Project in the Amazon rainforest to produce paper and cellulose. These products serve as an alternative to the widespread use of plastic, which has contributed to significant environmental damage globally. The Jari Project attracted thousands of poor settlers to the forest and formed a large area adjacent to a company town called Monte Dourado. Years later, the project expanded to include logging activities that followed eco-efficiency principles to prevent deforestation, employing selective cutting methods. The expansion was conducted in territory occupied by nut gatherers, a group who initially sought employment with the Jari Project, but when that opportunity fell through, many of them became peasants and turned to extracting Brazil nuts and other forest resources for a living.

Since the wood extraction required heavy machinery in the areas used for collecting nuts, the project conflicted with the traditional activity of gathering Brazil nuts, which used rustic technology to gather nuts and transport them for sale. Although the Brazil nut gatherers and the company do not dispute the same natural resources, the two extractive practices occurred in the same territory (legally classified as state land), albeit with different logics and goals—one market-driven and the other focused on livelihood, both authorized by the state.

Due to conflicting interests, in 2014, a community known as Repartimento dos Pilões organized human blockades, locally referred to as "empates," in the forest. These blockades prevented the company's machinery from entering the community-based Brazil nut gathering areas. This nonviolent strategy was inspired by the mobilizations of rubber tappers that took place decades earlier (discussed in greater detail below). While the strategy temporarily disrupted the company's activities, the conflict continued for many years. Even today, community members continue to struggle for their property title while also facing challenges from the corporate forest management project adjacent to their territory. This conflict has also obstructed negotiations with the state land authority, which is responsible for recognizing the Brazil nut gatherers' occupation and granting them the land title.[6]

The Repartimento dos Pilões case demonstrates how corporate appropriation of the eco-efficiency model can harm vulnerable communities in sensitive places like the Amazon rainforest. Environmental injustice can occur even when environmental management intentions seem benign toward the Natural World.

Socio-Environmentalism

Socio-environmentalism emerged from unabated deforestation in Abya Yala South (or South America), where immense forest regions inhabited by local communities have been converted into pastures and agricultural fields. Unlike the previous model, the socio-environmental perspective is community-centered and closely tied to the struggles of Latin American social movements that aim to promote the social, economic, and political empowerment of local communities. These communities rely on ongoing environmental conservation for their existence and to maintain their traditional lifestyles, which assume a symbiotic relationship with the land they inhabit and a closer connection to Nature.

Rubber Tappers

The rubber tappers are part of the local communities that initiated the socio-environmental movement. Many of them are impoverished settlers who migrated to the Amazon in the early twentieth century in search of jobs and better living conditions. Upon their arrival in the rainforest, they found work analogous to debt slavery—work rooted in cycles of indebtedness to landowners—where only a few workers could liberate themselves. During World War II, a second wave of immigration and rubber production began in the Amazon region when a daring Henry Ford launched a project to export rubber for the American automobile industry. Once more, many settlers were drawn to the Amazon rainforest. In these two waves of settlement, the Brazilian government encouraged workers from other regions of Brazil to relocate to Indigenous lands where rubber trees grow naturally. Although Ford's plantation project ultimately failed, the settlers chose to remain, and most never returned to their original homes.

In the 1980s, rubber tappers began adopting a socio-environmental strategy in their struggle for improved living conditions and the right to remain on the lands they occupied and considered home. They had already learned to maintain a harmonious relationship with Nature, partly through contact and assimilation with the Indigenous Peoples who lived in the rainforest. They integrated these lessons with the discourse of environmentalists, thereby appropriating that discourse for their own purposes. The result was a new framework for Nature protection and sustainability: ecological balance, low-impact production (using methods to produce goods from the forest that minimize harm to the environment), and community empowerment.

The rubber tappers' strategy also resulted in environmental conservation that integrates preservation with the presence of human communities, viewing people as inseparable from Nature. This contrasts with earlier waves of environmentalism that emphasized a separation between humans and the Natural World. This approach led to extractive reservations, which were inspired by, yet distinct from, the original Indigenous reservations. Extractive reservations are based on community-based and local interpretations of sustainability, centered around three conventional axes of sustainable development: the interplay of economic growth, environmental conservation, and social justice.

Unlike earlier waves of environmentalism, socio-environmentalists emphasize the multidimensionality of environmental issues. They highlight the importance of grassroots participation in political discussions about the environment, especially among those most directly affected by environmental harm. Consequently, rubber tappers and similar groups, such as Brazil nut gatherers, adopted comparable resistance strategies and devised innovative solutions to long-standing problems by integrating concerns about land, the environment, community empowerment, and nonviolent engagement within the forest.

In the quote that opens this chapter, Chico Mendes envisions these intersections when he asserts that "environmentalism without class struggle is gardening." His statement underscores that environmental protection involves social struggle; it entails more than simply reducing plastic consumption, hugging trees, contemplating waterfalls, loving pets, and cultivating gardens—even though those aspects matter too.

Postponing the End of the World

Settler environmentalism strategies have been utilized to ameliorate the numerous wounds from the First Harm and the environmental damage resulting from the illegal occupation of Indigenous lands. For Native women and men like Ailton Krenak, an Indigenous leader of the Krenak People, these settler strategies are merely temporary measures that "postpone the end of the world."[7] They divert attention away from the "fall of the sky," as taught by David Kopenawa, a Yanomami shaman from Brazil.[8]

While the settlers' romanticism regarding their role in protecting Nature warrants criticism, settler-led environmental movements—whether focused on climate change, community initiatives, market-driven eco-efficiency, or Nature conservation—are indeed necessary. These efforts mark a step toward restoring the broken relationship with the Natural World and collaborating with the First Environmentalists, the Indigenous Peoples. In the next chapter, we will explore alternative paths for protecting the environment within the US context, grounded in how Black people, Indigenous Peoples, and other People of Color understand environmental justice.

Chapter 3
Environmental Justice and Environmental Racism

We are saying that we are determined to be men. We are determined to be people. We are saying that we are God's children.
—Martin Luther King Jr.'s last speech, 1968

Alongside the environmentalist waves from white settlers, a non-white US-based model emerged from social struggles against the unequal distribution of environmental damages and hazards. This movement, known as environmental justice, is closely linked to racial struggles rooted in the Civil Rights Movement and led by Black, Indigenous, and other communities of color. Although Dr. King, Rosa Parks, and many other civil rights leaders did not use the term "environmental justice" in the way we know it today, the ecology movement took notice and began to incorporate ideas from the Civil Rights Movement.

After introducing the key civil rights event that ignited the movement, the chapter outlines environmental justice's main ideas, their close relationship with racial issues, and seventeen guiding principles. We conclude the chapter by examining the Mní Wičhóni (Water Is Life) movement against the Dakota Access Pipeline (DAPL) construction. This analysis highlights an Indigenous perspective on environmental justice that, while similar to other forms of environmental justice, provides unique contributions that promote a more multidimensional view of environmental protection.

The First Step: Memphis Sanitation Strikes

The environmental justice movement took its first major step in Memphis, Tennessee, during the sanitation strikes of the late 1960s. Garbage workers mobilized to denounce the unfair pay and degrading conditions they faced, particularly the unsafe work environments that led to the deaths of two sanitation workers, Echol Cole and Robert Walker. Both men were tragically crushed by a malfunctioning trash truck on February 1, 1968. In the wake of these deaths, Memphis garbage workers, predominantly Black people and other People of Color, came together and conducted daily peaceful marches through the streets, carrying signs that read, I AM A MAN.

Violent clashes with police erupted during these demonstrations. It was during this struggle that, hours after a speech supporting the sanitation workers, Martin Luther King Jr. was assassinated. Four days later, over 42,000 people marched silently through the streets of Memphis. Coretta Scott King, along with several religious and union leaders, led the march to honor the fallen leader of the Civil Rights Movement. Only then were the workers' demands recognized with a promise to fulfill them.

After the Memphis Sanitation Strikes, several additional mobilizations for environmental justice occurred. For example, in 1979, a group of African American homeowners in Houston, Texas, began a fierce fight to stop the Whispering Pines Sanitary Landfill, which was planned to be less than 1,500 feet from a local public school and under two miles from six other schools. In 1982, African Americans mobilized a broad-based national, nonviolent coalition to protest against a polychlorinated biphenyl (PCB) landfill in Warren County, North Carolina. More recently, Black Lives Matter, the global movement advocating for the rights of Black people, has also demonstrated that climate justice is inseparable from racial justice.[1]

Moreover, several foundational documents were produced. Among them, we highlight the 1987 report "Toxic Waste and Race in the United States," which was signed by Benjamin Chavis, an African American civil rights leader and ordained minister of the United Church of Christ, along with Charles Lee, a Taiwanese American environmental justice activist who later became a senior policy advisor in the Office of Environmental Justice at the US Environmental Protection Agency (EPA). This document, published by the United Church of Christ Commission for Racial Justice, was the first to denounce the link between the locations of hazardous waste facilities and the racial and ethnic makeup of surrounding communities.

Environmental Justice and Racism
Environmental justice denounces the fact that environment-related injustices are rooted in racism and

critiques the unequal distribution of adverse environmental impacts that disproportionately affect Black people, Indigenous People, and other People of Color, including Latinos, Pacific Islanders, and Asian Americans, as well as poor and working-class communities. The concept of "environmental racism" emerges from this awareness. Benjamin Chavis defined environmental racism as "racial discrimination in environmental policy-making, the enforcement of regulations and laws, the deliberate targeting of communities of colour for toxic waste facilities, the official sanctioning of the life-threatening presence of poisons and pollutants in our communities, and the history of excluding people of colour from [the] leadership of the ecology movements."[2] Therefore, environmental justice and environmental racism are practically conjoined twins; they cannot be understood separately without compromising the depth of the issues to which they refer.

At the same time, environmental justice has united with climate justice. Human-caused climate change and climate-related catastrophes are often empirically linked to racial and socioeconomic factors, disproportionately affecting groups with fewer resources to mitigate adverse climatic events.[3] Extreme natural events, such as recurring hurricanes in the Southeastern United States and along the Gulf of Mexico's coast, tend to inflict more severe damage on Black people and other People of Color. However, much of the climate change discourse complicates the connection between the damages caused by extreme climate events and racial issues. This discrepancy arises because climate change narratives often categorize everyone uniformly as victims of extreme climatic events. This approach frequently obscures the reality that, while everyone is impacted, they do not experience these events equally. Therefore, it is crucial to discuss climate justice in close relation to racial justice.

Principles of Environmental Justice

In October 1991, the multinational First People of Color Environmental Leadership Summit was held in Washington, DC. Nearly three hundred Black, Native, Latino, Pacific Islander, Asian American, and other marginalized activists gathered. They proposed and adopted seventeen principles of environmental justice (see text box). These principles highlight the core ideas and demands of environmental justice.

Principles of Environmental Justice

WE, THE PEOPLE OF COLOR, gathered together at this multinational People of Color Environmental Leadership Summit, to begin to build a national and international movement of all peoples of color to fight the destruction and taking of our lands and communities, do hereby re-establish our spiritual interdependence to the sacredness of our Mother Earth; to respect and celebrate each of our cultures, languages and beliefs about the natural world and our roles in healing ourselves; to ensure environmental justice; to promote economic alternatives which would contribute to the development of environmentally safe livelihoods; and, to secure our political, economic and cultural liberation that has been denied for over 500 years of colonization and oppression, resulting in the poisoning of our communities and land and the genocide of our peoples, do affirm and adopt these Principles of Environmental Justice:

1. Environmental justice affirms the sacredness of Mother Earth, ecological unity and the interdependence of all species, and the right to be free from ecological destruction.
2. Environmental justice demands that public policy be based on mutual respect and justice for all peoples, free from any form of discrimination or bias.
3. Environmental justice mandates the right to ethical, balanced and responsible uses of land and renewable resources in the interest of a sustainable planet for humans and other living things.
4. Environmental justice calls for universal protection from nuclear testing, extraction, production and disposal of toxic/hazardous wastes and poisons... that threaten the fundamental right to clean air, land, water, and food.
5. Environmental justice affirms the fundamental right to political, economic, cultural and environmental self-determination of all peoples.
6. Environmental justice demands the cessation of the production of all toxins, hazardous wastes, and radioactive materials, and that all past and current producers be held strictly accountable to the people for detoxification and the containment at the point of production.

7. Environmental justice demands the right to participate as equal partners at every level of decision-making including needs assessment, planning, implementation, enforcement and evaluation.
8. Environmental justice affirms the right of all workers to a safe and healthy work environment, without being forced to choose between an unsafe livelihood and unemployment. It also affirms the right of those who work at home to be free from environmental hazards.
9. Environmental justice protects the right of victims of environmental injustice to receive full compensation and reparations for damages as well as quality health care.
10. Environmental justice considers governmental acts of environmental injustice a violation of international law, the Universal Declaration on Human Rights, and the United Nations Convention on Genocide.
11. Environmental justice must recognize a special legal and natural relationship of Native Peoples to the US government through treaties, agreements, compacts, and covenants affirming sovereignty and self-determination.
12. Environmental justice affirms the need for urban and rural ecological policies to clean up and rebuild our cities and rural areas in balance with nature, honoring the cultural integrity of all our communities, and providing fair access for all to the full range of resources.
13. Environmental justice calls for the strict enforcement of principles of informed consent,

> and a halt to the testing of experimental reproductive and medical procedures and vaccinations on people of color.
> 14. Environmental justice opposes the destructive operations of multi-national corporations.
> 15. Environmental justice opposes military occupation, repression and exploitation of lands, peoples and cultures, and other life forms.
> 16. Environmental justice calls for the education of present and future generations which emphasizes social and environmental issues, based on our experience and an appreciation of our diverse cultural perspectives.
> 17. Environmental justice requires that we, as individuals, make personal and consumer choices to consume as little of Mother Earth's resources and to produce as little waste as possible; and make the conscious decision to challenge and reprioritize our lifestyles to insure the health of the natural world for present and future generations.[4]

Mní Wičhóni Movement: An Indigenous Perspective on Environmental Justice

The seventeen principles reveal how closely environmental justice aligns with the struggles of Indigenous Peoples from Abya Yala, in both North and South America. In the United States, they have fought against the settlers' destruction of their homelands since 1492. Despite public and international recognition of the significant contributions their cultures have made to environmental conservation, Indigenous Peoples remain among the most marginalized and continue to suffer the most from settler-led development.

We are fortunate, however, that their contributions continue to thrive. Although their resistance has characteristics that distinguish it from other environmental justice movements—such as the fact that Indigenous Peoples often do not use the term "environment" to define their struggles—it can be viewed as environmental justice in action. A notable example is the fight against the Dakota Access Pipeline (DAPL). The anti-DAPL movement sparked the most significant Indigenous mobilization against settler colonialism and environmental harm in nearly a century.

In the spring of 2016, a large Indigenous mobilization caught US society off guard. The Oyáte, commonly known to settlers as the Sioux Nation, with support from across the country, established community encampments to oppose the construction of the Dakota Access Pipeline. DAPL was a 1,172-mile underground oil pipeline running from North Dakota to a terminal in Illinois, crossing areas near the Standing Rock Sioux Tribe's territory and other treaty lands. The pipeline posed adverse environmental risks in at least four US states, impacting two major rivers and their tributaries. This environmental action, referred to by its participants as the Mní Wičhóni Movement (MWM or Water is Life movement), revealed long-standing settler wrongdoing: invading and occupying Indigenous Peoples' lands without their consent. The pipeline violated treaties ratified by American settlers, which stipulated that, to resolve violent conflicts between settlers and the Oyáte, the United States promised not to trespass on Sioux Nation lands without their free, prior, and informed consent.

The original DAPL route did not trespass on any contested treaty land. However, it was altered to avoid areas primarily inhabited by white settlers, thereby shielding them from any environmental damage and hazards associated with DAPL. On its revised route, DAPL approached the Mní Šoše Wakpá (also known as the Missouri River) to the south, away from the concentration of white settlers.

The Oyáte understand that the Mní Oyáte (the Water Nation) flowing in this river is a living being with attributes that humans can recognize. They share the same Creation story and source of energy, or Creation's blood. Therefore, the Oyáte and Mní Oyáte see each other as peoples and blood relatives. Creation's foundational teaching requires them to be mutually good relatives to one another, and, of course, to avoid harming each other. The construction of an oil pipeline that crosses the river is not only about violating treaties, the risk of leaks, and danger to Indigenous lives; it also concerns the sacredness of a beloved relative that must be protected from harm. Thus, the Oyáte see themselves as protectors, not protesters, with their encampments acting as a protective measure—a human shield.

The construction of DAPL exemplifies environmental racism. Although it did not stop the pipeline's construction, the Mní Wičhóni Movement stands out for its extensive scope, duration, number of people involved, social media engagement, and the Oyáte's nonviolent resistance tactics and strategies. Overall, the MWM reminded American settlers of the long-standing harm and ongoing claims of the

Oyáte and other Indigenous Peoples resulting from settler colonialism. More importantly, the MWM provided a lesson about how Indigenous Peoples understand their relationship with other-than-human beings and what it means to be a relative to the Natural World. It represented the unique Indigenous way of protecting and fighting for environmental justice, encompassing the rights and personhood of the Natural World, as well as treaty rights, human rights, and self-determination.

Standing with the Environment Together

The struggles of Indigenous, Black, and other communities of color, alongside poor and working-class communities, have undoubtedly shaped environmentalist frameworks that are more multidimensional than those of the white settlers. These frameworks acknowledge that environmental justice encompasses psychological, relational, social, economic, political, cultural, ecological, and spiritual dimensions, necessitating complex approaches to prevent and address environmental harm and injustice.

Our intention in describing them is not to deny the value of settler environmentalism frameworks. On the contrary, all waves of environmentalism—whether conceived by white or non-white groups—are important and should not be arbitrarily dismissed. They complement each other and can help us develop the necessary strategies to tackle our current environmental issues. Together, they offer lessons that can lead people to change the unsustainable path we are on and, perhaps, bring an end to the ecological crisis that has been escalating since colonization began. Having described MWM as an Indigenous struggle for environmental justice, the next chapter will deepen the discussion on the Indigenous understanding of the Natural World and its contribution to environmentalism.

Chapter 4
Restoring the Broken Kinship

We need to unforget our histories and the relationships they contain. We need to become kin.[1]
—Patty Krawec

Growing environmental awareness in recent decades has sparked a heightened interest in Indigenous Peoples' wisdom regarding the Natural World, particularly their traditional ecological knowledge (TEK). Unquestionably, Native Peoples possess worldviews that suggest a reciprocal relationship between humanity and Nature. Settler societies could learn a great deal from these worldviews, which contrast sharply with the settler perspective on the environment. Some environmentalists contend that revitalizing Indigenous TEKs could better prevent and address harmful climatic events. This chapter introduces the Indigenous understanding of the relationship with the Natural World, drawing on examples from Abya Yala North and South.

We begin by exploring the connection between settler colonialism and the 2025 California wildfires, a severe natural disaster that took place in the Southwestern United States. We shift our attention to TEK, particularly the Karuk People's experience with "good fires" (or controlled burns) and two important aspects of Native worldviews regarding the Natural World: Nature as a People and the kinship between humans and other-than-human beings. We conclude by inviting readers to reflect on how we can make things right after the wildfires by becoming good relatives to Nature and embracing what is known as "good living"—an Indigenous ethic centered on harmonious coexistence with all living beings.

Wildfires in California: Settler Colonialism and Disruption of TEK

At the start of 2025, California experienced a series of devastating wildfires, which particularly impacted the Los Angeles area. These fires claimed dozens of lives and destroyed thousands of homes and other structures. Many individuals evacuated quickly, uncertain if they would have anything to return home to. The fires received national and international media coverage, considering their impact on Hollywood, the film industry's calendar (such as delaying news about Oscar nominations), and the lives of many celebrities.

While wildfires in California occur almost every year, the intensity in 2025 was unprecedented. The recurrence of these extreme events has become a significant environmental issue. A question arises: "Why were the wildfires so severe this time?" As widely discussed in the media, the weather undoubtedly played a crucial role. California experienced eight months without rain, leaving trees and grasses dry and primed for ignition. Powerful winds accelerated the flames' spread. Climate change is also driving the rising frequency and intensity of wildfires. These fires release carbon into the atmosphere without restraint, further accelerating climate change and making certain landscapes more susceptible to recurring wildfires. In general, climate change has led to an increase in uncontrollable wildfires, whether triggered by human activities or natural events.

But this was not all. Not everyone knows, and many choose to forget, that wildfires are deeply rooted in settlers' disruption of Indigenous environmental stewardship practices and the imposition of settler land-use systems. The connection between these two settler actions has had lasting effects on fire regimes in vulnerable landscapes.

Disruption of TEK

Some Indigenous Peoples have practiced cultural burning for thousands of years to manage their forests. These controlled burns reduced fuel buildup, maintained biodiversity, and sustained food and medicinal plant resources. When settlers arrived in Abya Yala, they viewed these practices, along with other Indigenous wisdom, as wasteful and even dangerous. Policies such as the Indian Government and Protection Act of 1850—enacted by the first session of the California State Legislature and signed into law by California's first Governor, Peter Hardeman Burnett—criminalized Indigenous burning. This repression led to unchecked vegetation growth, which increased wildfires over time.

Moreover, the forced removal of Indigenous Peoples from their homelands has disrupted traditional ecological knowledge practices, such as cultural burning. As if this were not enough, the regulatory framework established by settler governments often erases Indigenous voices in fire management. Indeed, Indigenous Peoples face legal barriers to conducting controlled burns, even as state and federal agencies begin to acknowledge the value of TEK.

Settler Land Use
Settlers have prioritized the extraction of natural resources, such as logging and mining, along with monoculture agriculture and cattle ranching. Clear-cutting forests has eliminated fire-resistant old growth, leaving behind flammable young trees. This approach to land development has decreased landscape resilience and made fires increasingly destructive, even for humans. Land privatization and fragmentation have complicated fire management, resulting in a patchwork of fire-prone properties with limited coordination for prevention.

It is evident that wildfires are directly connected to settler colonialism and the neglect of traditional fire stewardship practices. Returning to Indigenous traditional knowledge can mitigate wildfire risks and potentially remedy the environmental damage settlers have caused. The concept of "good fires" could teach us how to repair our relationship with the Natural World.

"Good Fires": Partnering with Fire Kin
The documentary *Inhabitants: Indigenous Perspectives on Restoring Our World* tells stories about how Native Peoples have stewarded diverse landscapes for millennia, even amid the settlers' disruption of their

TEK, and have revitalized their ancient relationships with the Natural World. Utilizing a pun often shared by Howard Zehr in discussions of restorative justice, Indigenous Peoples are "re-storying" a kinship with the Natural World that settler colonialism fractured. One notable example of this re-storying is that of the Karuk People, Indigenous to a corner of California, who have mobilized their efforts to revitalize an ancestral relationship with Fire.

Like other nonhuman beings, Fire is regarded as a beloved relative. The settlers, however, transformed this relative into an enemy to be extinguished. Therefore, the Karuk needed to return to their concept of "pikyav," which means "to fix it,"[2] or, as stated on the Karuk Tribe's website, the daily "efforts to restore the earth and its creatures to a harmonious balance."

Pikyav is ancestral knowledge transmitted intergenerationally through the Karuk's traditional stories, which have been told since time immemorial. These stories "recount the formation of plants, aquatic species, land formations, and other resources created and given to us to utilize and manage."[3] This TEK recognizes Karuk's responsibilities to other-than-human beings. Violating these obligations can disrupt the Natural World, and the ensuing damage may, in turn, return to humans as a consequence of their wrongdoing. Arguably, uncontrollable wildfires are a natural response to human violations.

It is necessary, therefore, to repair the damage already caused and, above all, rebuild the relationship between humans and the Natural World. One way to do this is by relearning and practicing Indigenous ways of forest stewardship.

The Karuk Peoples thus practice pikyav with their Fire relative. Rather than instilling fear, Fire rejuvenates life for the Karuk and other Indigenous Peoples. The Karuk People have historically utilized cultural burns, or "good fires" (also known as controlled burns), to sustain forest health, mitigate wildfires, and safeguard places humans and other-than-humans inhabit. By periodically burning brush and dry vegetation, the Karuk reduces the fuel loads that can lead to devastating wildfires. This practice establishes firebreaks and prevents the buildup of dangerous conditions.

Bill Tripp, the Director of Natural Resources and Environmental Policy at the Karuk Tribe Department of Natural Resources, explains that such burns are cultural practices "developed by people who have been in a place a very long time, who know their surroundings intimately and know that you need to do specific things at specific times for a reason, so when it's time, you just go do it,"[4] and are "based on a consistent application of standard principles."[5] They reflect deep ecological knowledge and emphasize the balance between humans and the Natural World.

Settler colonialism weakened this reciprocal relationship with the Natural World, and Fire is one of the other-than-humans from whom we have drifted away. Despite this, many settlers nostalgically recall how people would gather around fires to warm themselves, celebrate, tell stories, engage in dialogue, laugh, mourn, make peace, hold ceremonies, and heal. Why? For thousands of years, Fire protected us from predators and helped ensure the continuity of human life. Fire has contributed to cooking food, purifying water, clearing grounds, making habitable areas viable, and preparing soil for agriculture. Fire has long warmed our lives, especially during cold weather, and played a crucial role in ceremonial practices and religious services in both Indigenous and settler societies. Last but not least, as the Karuk's "good fires" remind us, Fire is a partner in preventing massive, destructive fires.

"The Environment" Is People

To understand that Fire is a partner in fighting fires, one must grasp how some Indigenous Peoples of Abya Yala North and South understand their relationship with the Natural World. For some, this relationship may seem peculiar, or there may be misconceptions, especially regarding what settlers refer to as "the environment." For Native ecological knowledge to be understood, it is necessary to open our minds to Indigenous worldviews.

At the risk of being quite reductionist, we could say that Indigenous Peoples understand all living beings with whom we coexist—animals, plants, waters, rocks, hills, mountains, fire, and so on—as having personhood no different from that of any human being. In other words, nonhumans are Peoples; they have nations, clans, communities, or tribes. Thus, like humans, the Natural World beings possess agency, worth, dignity, and rights. Indeed, unlike the settlers' concerns about environmental conservation and justice, the ecological ethic of Indigenous Peoples is based on what humans do *with*—and not *to*—"the environment."

Indigenous Peoples recognize distinctions between humans and other-than-humans, but not to the extent settlers imagine. We are discussing distinct—albeit related—living beings. For Indigenous Peoples, however, there is no belief in human superiority over other-than-humans. Instead, there are relationships or bidirectional exchanges of matter and energy between humanity and other living beings. These exchanges rely on reciprocity and trust.[6] As a result, the Natural World should be engaged with, not dominated.[7] The Oyáte (United States), Achuar (Ecuador), and Cree (Canada) all exemplify this engagement.

Oyáte and Wakkíŋyaŋ Aglípi

Around every spring equinox, the Oyáte gather at a particular site to welcome the return of a relative: Wakkíŋyaŋ Aglípi (Thunder Beings Came Back).

> Ceremonially, when the sun is in the Wičhíŋčala Šakówiŋ constellation, the people know to Welcome-Back-The-Thunders. . . . This communal ceremony coincides with the Spring Equinox, and it signals to the people to start making preparations for upcoming summer ceremonies. These timed ceremonies ensure that the people will continue on, stay connected to each other, and are thankful to the Natural World.[8]

As this quote illustrates, the Thunder Beings are welcomed relatives who return during a particular time of year and are ceremonially greeted for a renewed cycle.

Achuar and Hunting Animals

The Achuar, an Indigenous people living in the Ecuadorian Amazon, acknowledge that animals possess social institutions analogous to those of humans and that animals view their species members as a community. Other species are seen as tribes, featuring group leaders and sharing equal or indistinguishable status with human hunters. The Achuar often negotiate mutually beneficial arrangements with these other-than-human people. For these Indigenous people, animals give of themselves—through their flesh, skin, and bones—in the act of hunting, which holds significant meaning. The Achuar honor and pray to the spirits that oversee the hunting grounds, demonstrating their respect for the Natural World. They take only what is necessary for the family or community, ensuring they do not exploit or violate other-than-human beings.[9]

Cree and the Caribou

The Cree, who live in northeastern Canada, provide another example. When a Cree hunter finds himself facing a caribou, an exchange often occurs. At a certain point, the caribou becomes aware of the Cree's presence, and instead of running, it freezes. This behavior gives a significant advantage to the hunter, who can easily take down the prey. The Cree people understand that a caribou's willingness to give itself up arises from a spirit of goodwill, love, trust, and mutuality. This understanding illustrates the continuity of the relatedness between the Cree and the Caribou People.[10] Indeed, many Indigenous Peoples perform ceremonies before and after hunting. They express gratitude to other-than-human peoples who sacrifice themselves on behalf of their Indigenous relatives.

Indigenous relationships with the Natural World, as demonstrated in these three examples, reflect a circular order in which humans and other-than-humans are interdependent and engaged in the reciprocal relationships necessary to ensure balance on the planet. As the white philosopher Leonardo Boff said, there is a "tendency of ecosystems towards dynamic balance, cooperation and co-evolution, and accounts for the interdependencies of all with all, ensuring the inclusion of each, even the weakest."[11] Despite what we have been taught to believe, humans are part of ecosystems and must act sustainably. We are only outside of the Natural World if we remain strangers to it.

> ### Circle of Life
>
> As a child, I remember my mother speaking of the relationship all people have with the Land. She talked about how we moved with the Land and creation, and that all things move in a circle. She talked about the rounds of life and how we moved with the animals. We spent the spring near the rivers for fish and beaver, then moved to the lakes and marshes for the berries and lake fish, and then to the mountains to harvest the larger animals and put up food for the winter, then the valleys for the fur-bearing animals. This she referred to as the rounds of life, that all people make the rounds of life. Our life goes from entrance into this world from the spirit world through the stages of life until we return to the spirit world. This is known as the Circle of Life.[12]
>
> —Mark Wedge, a member of the Carcross/Tagish First Nation (Yukon Territory, Canada)

We Are All Relatives

As shown above, Indigenous worldviews emphasize that we, as humans, are deeply and holistically interconnected with everything and everyone around us, including other-than-human beings. No one should be excluded or left behind. The Oyáte model this way of life at their gatherings when they say Mitákuye Oyás'iŋ (All My Relatives). This Lakȟóta/Dakȟóta/Nakȟóta phrase signifies that all humans, animals, plants, waters, soil, stones, mountains, grasslands, winds, clouds, storms, the sun, moon, stars, and more are interconnected and, above all, related to one another. Often recited in prayer and ceremony, it acknowledges the interconnectedness of all things and conveys that we are all relatives. Kinship is not confined to humans; it extends to the Natural World.

Therefore, for Indigenous Peoples, environmental protection involves maintaining a mutual relatedness so that their behavior and lifeway do not fracture or harm the Natural World. If relatedness is fractured and the Natural World is harmed, protection strategies must work to repair or undo the harm. For this reason, people should stand up to defend the Natural World when it is threatened, as seen with water protectors and land defenders. This approach also entails returning to ancestral wisdom, which forms the roots of many TEK practices, such as the "good fires."[13]

The Good Living: An Indigenous Ethic

We return to the California wildfires and ask what we can do "after the wildfires spread." Viewed through an Indigenous worldview, the answer is to repair our relationship with the Natural World. Indeed, it is challenging to restore relationships after harm, whether that harm arises from human actions or natural events. White Professor Ben Almassi, in *Reparative Environmental Justice in a World of Wounds*, says that to restore these relationships, we must build a moral philosophy that comes "after the dam breaks." In other words, we need to reestablish the moral relationship that was broken in the aftermath of damage. In the context of the California wildfires, this means restoring relationships after the wildfires have spread. Inspired by the work of Margaret Walker—a settler philosopher dedicated to repairing moral relations after wrongdoing—Almassi refers to the amending response as "moral repair."[14]

For the Oyáte and other Indigenous Peoples of Abya Yala North, moral reparation involves returning to being good relatives with the Natural World and restoring kinship with other-than-human beings. Using a term from Abya Yala South, we can say that Indigenous Peoples seek "good living" with themselves, others, and Nature. This good living ethic is known as *sumak kawsay* in Kíchwa; *suma qamaña* in Aymara, *nhandereko* or *teko porã* in Guarani, *shiir waras* for the Achuar, and *küme mongen* for the Mapuche, to name just five of many terms for good living.[15] In other words, good living means living as good relatives with all living beings with whom we coexist.

Experiencing a good life is no easy task in settler-colonial contexts. Settler colonialism has sidelined the ancestral wisdom of Indigenous Peoples, resulting in the loss or marginalization of vital understandings about relationality. However, the extreme natural events and climate change we face today demand a more pluralistic world—one where diverse worldviews, including Indigenous perspectives, can coexist and learn from one another. For this to happen, settlers and Indigenous Peoples must recognize each other as relatives, and the Natural World must be seen in the same light. While we know this is a challenging task, the next chapter explores how peacemaking circles and the Oyáte's worldview—centered on turning strangers into relatives—may provide a path forward.

Chapter 5
Making Strangers Relatives

Why would you take from us by force that which you may obtain by love?
—Powhatan's reply to John Smith, 1609

In 1609, Powhatan, speaking for a confederacy of several Indigenous nations, directly asked the settlers: "Why would you take from us by force that which you may obtain by love?" From the Oyáte's viewpoint, when Powhatan presented settlers with a different way based on love, he was reaching out to make them relatives. We can appreciate that he proposed restoring the relationships that had been fractured since the very onset of colonization in Abya Yala. However, since we are not descendants of Powhatan's People, we cannot claim to know the precise nature of the love Powhatan offered the settlers.

Nonetheless, Oyáte thought and philosophy invite us to consider a love so profound that we appreciate the "what-ifs." What if settlers, both now and in the future, could obtain what they need to live through love, not violence? What if settlers chose restorative paths to deal with the issues that entangle them with Indigenous Peoples? What if settlers and Indigenous Peoples embraced one another as relatives and acted with love toward each other? Even posing these deep moral questions can have a restorative effect.

You may wonder what these making-of-relatives and love sensibilities have to do with restorative justice and the environment. This chapter examines that wonder. We begin by sharing a story about peacemaking circles used to address a conflict involving settlers and Indigenous Peoples. This story sets the stage for a discussion on restorative justice and circles, the way that Indigenous teachings have influenced their development, and their potential for making strangers relatives. We then present Oyáte's kinship-based perspective on relationships, which is central to the idea of transforming strangers into relatives, and its roots in love, not force. We conclude by revisiting Powhatan's inquiry about love and its connection to being a good relative.

"This Is the Justice We Want"

On a July 2019 morning, the Amazon Restorative Justice Clinic at the Federal University of Western Pará received a phone call from the prosecutor's office. The prosecutor, a white settler, informed the program that a physical altercation had occurred involving Indigenous and non-Indigenous adolescents. An Arapiun youth had assaulted a white youth after being bullied about his ethnicity. This incident caused the non-Indigenous teenager to faint on the soccer field near the community school. Subsequently, relatives of the white adolescent chased the Indigenous boy, even injuring the aunt with whom he lived. Although the usual procedure in such situations was to initiate prosecution, the prosecutor opted for an alternative approach: a peacemaking circle. The first restorative justice circle was conducted on that day to begin addressing the case.

Two circle keepers—one settler and one Indigenous member from the Kumaruara, a neighboring Indigenous People—went to the prosecutor's office to facilitate the process. This first circle included the Indigenous adolescent who caused the harm, an aunt responsible for him, the father and mother of the white teenager who was harmed, and Indigenous and non-Indigenous people from the community, as well as a teacher from the school where both adolescents were enrolled and two community leaders. The non-Indigenous adolescent did not participate because his parents had not taken him with them to the prosecutor's office. The facilitators invited everyone to discuss what had happened, who was harmed, who was responsible for the harm, how to make things right, and how to prevent similar incidents in the future. The discussion helped people understand what led to and resulted from the altercation, as well as the involved parties' responsibilities, which were perceived as shared rather than solely individual. The participants collectively decided that a second circle should be held. Just over a month later, the same individuals gathered with other Indigenous and non-Indigenous community members, including relatives of both the white teenager—who participated this time—and the Indigenous adolescent.

Across these two circles, the responsibility of the Indigenous adolescent was examined, and the complexities of what happened and the shared responsibilities emerged. Let us explore a few examples. Following the soccer field incident, the white teenager's relatives reacted violently toward the Indigenous adolescent. This reaction caused lasting physical harm to the Indigenous adolescent's aunt, who injured her leg while attempting to defend her nephew and prevent the white teenager's relatives from forcibly entering her home. Participants in the circle discussed the responsibility these white relatives bore for the harm they inflicted on the adolescent and his aunt.

The circle was an opportunity to let everybody know about the vulnerable situation of the Indigenous adolescent. He had endured considerable violence at home from his stepfather, a non-Indigenous man, with whom he and his mother lived, albeit outside their homeland. This violence prompted him to leave his mother's house in Santarém, a midsize city in the Amazon region, and return to the village where other relatives lived. After discussing this situation, both the Indigenous and non-Indigenous community members present committed to support the Indigenous adolescent emotionally and in relation to community reintegration, school attendance, and cultural and work activities. This community support aimed to strengthen his resilience before he faced any risk factors, ultimately helping to prevent further harmful incidents.

The circle allowed the white teenager to express his feelings and thoughts about the harmful event while also addressing the responsibility of those who harassed the Indigenous adolescent through ethnicity-related bullying. It served as a safe, respectful, and nonviolent space for the community to discuss violence and racism against Indigenous Peoples and how divisions along ethnic lines between Indigenous and non-Indigenous individuals set the stage for the conflict between the two adolescents. Participants in the circle also discussed concerns regarding the ongoing impact of the conflict at school, where Indigenous and non-Indigenous students had to coexist despite their ethnic differences.

Ultimately, the participants agreed that the Indigenous adolescent responsible for the damage could remain in the village. He would receive support from his relatives, which would help protect him, decrease his vulnerability, and build resilience. The Indigenous adolescent apologized to the white teenager and promised not to commit similar acts in the future. The white teenager also received support from his relatives and other community members and committed to respecting Indigenous Peoples, especially the Indigenous adolescent who caused harm.

Following the circles, Auricélia Arapiun, a leader from the Arapiun People, stated: "This is the justice we want!" After the restorative justice process, she informed the circle keepers that the white teenager and the Indigenous adolescent, along with their families, had become good relatives despite the tensions they had experienced in the past.[1]

This case shows both how conflicts between settlers and Indigenous people can resonate in adolescents and the difficulty of establishing a good life within the framework of settler colonialism. Indeed, this conflict occurred in São Pedro Village, located in the Tapajós-Arapiuns Extractive Reservation in the Amazon region of Brazil where settlers and Indigenous people experience numerous conflicts, including around land use. Yet, the circles brought together the two ethnically distinct groups and advanced their common interests in promoting good living. They show that the circles not only addressed the conflict among the adolescents but also the underlying structural problem related to the division between settlers and Indigenous Peoples. As such, the circles exposed the multidimensional nature of and response to harm and offered a way for settlers and Indigenous Peoples to make one another relatives.

Restorative Justice and Circles

Though forged in settler societies, Indigenous ways of addressing harm and wrongdoing have inspired contemporary restorative justice. Thus, we can argue that the dialogue between the settlers and Indigenous Peoples revolves around the question of "What does justice look like?" The late white Professor Elizabeth Elliott explains restorative justice this way:

> In restorative justice, the response to harm is motivated not by the quest for punitive consequences for individual offenders, but for healing of each individual affected by the harm as well as the collective healing of the community in which the harm occurred.[2]

As seen in the São Pedro Village case, circles can foster safe spaces for participants to talk about how they felt and were impacted by a harmful act, or oppressive structures that discriminate among people and groups based on ethnicity, race, gender, inequity, capability, and so on. Circles are a way to restore relationships that have been broken and rebuild the sense of community forgotten or harmed by a wrongdoing. At the same time, circles provide an opportunity to address harm in a multifaceted way, as they focus not only on the harmful incident itself but also on the various aspects involved in the issue at hand.

Like other restorative justice approaches, circles do not aim to punish but to gather people in search of healing after a harm. Kay Pranis, a white settler and prominent trainer advocating for circles globally, values a circle's potential to address difficult issues collectively through reliance on individual and collective wisdom. They adopt a holistic perspective, focused on the interconnectedness of all things, including the Natural World. Following traditional Indigenous knowledge, circles encourage participants to treat each other as good relatives, based on common values and shared guidelines built collectively.[3]

Howard Zehr once described restorative justice as a river with many tributaries, where different waters flow toward a common point. The peacemaking circle approach is a tributary that plays a crucial role in the broader history of restorative justice. Peacemaking circles are distinctive for being an approach rooted in an Indigenous vision of justice, originating from Abya Yala North, but also found in Abya Yala South.[4]

Peacemaking Circles: An Indigenous Story

To understand the story of the peacemaking circle and its influence on restorative justice, let us listen to Harold Gatensby, a member of the Carcross/Tagish First Nation who lives in Yukon Territory, Canada. He recounts the contemporary origins of settlers' contact with the circle process. Gatensby's story is distinctive because it portrays the settlers' quest for justice through the settler-imposed criminal justice system as failing and negatively affecting colonized Peoples.

> One day many years ago, a judge named Barry Stuart approached me on a circuit court day [once every two months] in Carcross and asked if I knew anything that could help make a difference. He was tired of seeing the same people in front of him in court over and over again, and he asked me if I knew of anything that could help. I responded without hesitation that I did. The judge then started making a training plan to prepare people to participate. He said how about we do some training and start in six months. My response to the judge was that we needed to start that very day. We wanted to introduce the circle ceremony to the courts, and we already knew it would have a positive impact. Reluctantly the judge agreed.
>
> We went out in the community and invited people to come and participate in our circle community court. About twenty-five people from our community of around three hundred showed up at the courts, and we began our circle sentencing process. The community was given a voice in the justice institution, and it made a positive difference for all that participated. Our community sentenced the first participants of circle court, and we sentenced two men to give something back to our community for their offenses.
>
> We, as a community, also realized that these men and others needed support so we started

> a community circle working group to support a healthier community. Our circle support group started to meet on a weekly basis and did some incredible work toward a healthier future for us all. All the work the community did was volunteer, and we worked hard. We worked with the police, we worked with the probation people, we worked with the prosecutors, we worked with the victims and offenders, we worked with the families, and all were welcome to participate. Our community built a working relationship with the people in the institutions.
>
> Our community working group looked back after four years of working together and realized we had reduced recidivism by about 85 percent and had sent no young offenders in the courts for four years, something we should all be proud of as a Community.[5]

Kay Pranis and Barry Stuart (both settlers), with input from Mark Wedge, a member of the Carcross/Tagish First Nation and a peacemaking circles trainer, synthesized an Indigenous-inspired circle approach to address wrongdoing and harm with the following principles:

- Provides an inclusive and community-based way of justice
- Seeks consensual decision-making on how to deal with behaviors that violate people and relationships
- Focuses not only on the past but also on the present and future

- Brings a perspective of shared responsibility to meet the needs of all people involved
- Keeps the person who caused harms within the community, if possible
- Addresses damages and healing traumas caused to the victim
- Provides support to those who need it
- Rescues people's trust by listening to their stories
- Uses collaborative procedures to find solutions
- Aims for outcomes that promote mutual benefits[6]

Though the above principles are Indigenous-*inspired*, they incorporate some settler assumptions and do not fully and exactly reflect Indigenous community practices. Nonetheless, they serve as a compass for those striving to transform settler justice systems toward humanizing, democratic, and inclusive models.

Carolyn Boyes-Watson, a white settler professor, stated that the Tlingit/Tagish People "gifted" circles to the restorative justice movement.[7] Although gifts are a traditional way to show others that we want to be with them in good relationships, both in Indigenous and settler societies, we must be skeptical about circles being a "gift" from Indigenous Peoples to settlers; failing to do so would normalize the subtle ways settlers typically appropriate Indigenous traditional knowledge.

However, we agree with Boyes-Watson when she says that Indigenous Peoples have modeled peacemaking circles with the hope that settlers might learn a way of relating to one another that contrasts with settlers' institutionalized, arrogant, hierarchical, and controlling patterns that have caused so much suffering to Indigenous communities. To rephrase her statement, we could say that Indigenous Peoples have showed circles as a way for strangers to become relatives. Whether this transformation, which is so desperately needed, happens remains an open question.

Making Strangers into Relatives

To more deeply explore the idea of transforming strangers into relatives, we introduce you to the late Ella Deloria from the Oyáte, who authored *Speaking of Indians*.[8] She describes Dakȟóta culture as "a scheme of life that works." For Deloria, relationships form the bedrock of belonging, the core to human survival. She states:

> All Dakota were held together in a great relationship that was theoretically all-inclusive and co-extensive with the Dakota domain. Everyone who was born a Dakota belonged in it; nobody needs [to] be left outside. This meant that the Dakota were no haphazard assemblages of heterogeneous individuals.[9]

To the uninitiated, Deloria's remark on inclusivity appears self-evident. Yet she reminds us that the Dakȟóta have found a way to get along with others, including non-Dakȟóta. Deloria elaborates:

> The dictates of kinship demanded of relatives that they not harm each other; so it was necessary first to make relatives of erstwhile strangers, thus putting them "on the spot," and then

deal with them on that basis. You assumed that as relatives they would be trustworthy, and by the same token you obligated yourself.[10]

In its broadest sense, Deloria's use of "kinship" and "relatives" is particularly instructive, especially as it relates to making "erstwhile strangers" relatives. From a Dakȟóta viewpoint, strangers are unpredictable. Dakȟóta concerns are unlike modern settlers' "Stranger Danger!" xenophobia. Instead, they want relatedness, but it is necessary to know how to do this based on a relationship's distinctive qualities. The Oyáte have at least thirty-six core kinship terms, with each signifying a reciprocal relationship within their broader community circle. Being Oyáte comes with intimately knowing who your relatives are, the proper ways to address them, and how to interact with them appropriately—and they with you. For instance, the Oyáte differentiate between three types of "aunt": one term for the father's sister, another for the mother's sister, and a third for the partner of the mother's brother.

Deloria notes that Dakȟóta customs distinguish between relatives, which also demands using the appropriate kinship term and corresponding behavior, which varies across relationships. She teaches that the essence of relationality involves "a proper mental attitude and a proper conventional behavior prescribed by kinship must accompany the speaking of each term." This prescription means that when you say "uncle" or "aunt," "father" or "mother," "brother" or "sister," "nephew" or "niece," kinship invites you into a relationship with him or her. So, "you must assume the correct mental attitude due to that particular relative addressed and you must express that attitude in its fitting outward behavior and mien [manner], according to [the] accepted convention."[11]

Being a stranger outside the kinship scheme means we cannot know your intentions, what to expect from you, or how to be a reciprocating relative. Therefore, strangers are unpredictable, and as Deloria illustrated, that unpredictability unnerves us.

One can transition from being a stranger to becoming a relative. This is a life-transforming process. The Oyáte understand these life-transforming processes as existing in one state while self-transforming into another. For example, an apple seed undergoes a transformation when it grows into an apple tree, just as a pumpkin seed transforms when it becomes a pumpkin or a grass seed changes as it grows into grass. Making strangers into relatives might seem trite to the uninitiated, akin to an apple seed growing into a tree. While we cannot fully explore the profound essence of transformation in Oyáte culture, one essential point remains: The self-transformation of strangers into relatives requires deliberate intent and actions to become a relative and to ensure no harm occurs.

When Deloria talks about putting people "on the spot," she means knowing what to expect in reciprocating behavior. Invoking appropriate kinship terms with their associated behavior eliminates unpredictability. Every Dakȟóta individual, regardless of age or gender, knew where they stood in relationships with others (and they to him or her). The Oyáte internalized a fundamental teaching from this custom: a relative does no harm.

Dakȟóta kinship supports people in being good relatives. Deloria elaborated on this moral imperative to being a good relative:

No Dakota who has participated in that life will dispute that. In the last analysis[,] every other consideration was secondary—property, personal ambition, glory, good times, [and] life itself. Without that aim and the constant struggle to attain it, the people would no longer be Dakota in truth. They would no longer be human.[12]

Other Indigenous Peoples share comparable views on relationality and how it plays out in Native communities, emphasizing the obligation of doing no harm. For instance, Chief Justice Robert Yazzie, a Diné (Navajo) citizen, employs the figurative "you" and remarks:

If you act as if you have no relatives, that [the harm] may come to you. . . . The Holy People created human beings. Due to that fact, each must respect others. One cannot harm another. If so, harm will come back on you. There are always consequences from wrongful acts, just as good comes from good.[13]

These duties and responsibilities are customary or common laws that guide collective relations and relationships among the Diné People.

Yazzie describes someone who violates Diné customary law as acting as if he or she has no relatives.[14] When a community member behaves this way, the Indigenous community has several options: they may either shun the violator or banish the violator from the community. Shunning serves as a warning to the violator that their actions have caused significant harm, urging them to strive to become a good relative once more. If shunning fails, banishment from the community severs relationships to the extent that the violator is left without any relatives. They become alienated from the community, which is a severe punishment for an Indigenous individual.

While settlers may view this form of Indigenous justice as retributive, it fundamentally differs from settler criminal justice. The Arapiun People case and Gatensby's story illustrate that Indigenous justice aims for inclusion and community restoration. Its main focus is to help a community member regain their status as a good relative. Thus, peacemaking circles prioritize values before delving into key issues, because the harmful actions represent a deviation from being a good relative. Consequently, rectifying these wrongs begins with exploring what it means to live in good conviviality. So, circles facilitate dialogues on difficult topics and aid the individual's reintegration into their social network or community.

It's About Love

Let us return to Powhatan's centuries-old question—"Why would you take from us by force that which you may obtain by love?"—and tweak it to say: "Why would *we* take from *each other* by force that which *we* may obtain by love?" Herein lies a road map for restorative justice.

Even today, love remains the alternative to violence. For instance, the late bell hooks,[15] an African American author, in her book, *All About Love: New Visions*, offers noteworthy guideposts for undoing violence in settler-colonial settings:

- Love and abuse cannot coexist;

- Domination cannot exist where a love ethic prevails;
- Without justice, there can be no love.[16]

These points reflect Indigenous Peoples' worldview of being good relatives, where once-estranged individuals become a relative and commit to do no harm, as Deloria instructs. In a 2000 NPR interview, hooks asserted that love, when embraced or accepted, can create a better world:

> People want to feel more connected. They want to feel more connected to their neighbors. They want to feel more connected to the world, and when we learn that through love we can have that connection, *we can see the stranger as ourselves.*[17]

Powhatan offered settlers this "we-can-see-the-stranger-as-ourselves"—a profound connection for anyone needing our love. hooks perhaps provided an alternative for undoing settler harms so we might better understand the kind of love Powhatan extended to them over four hundred years ago. She wrote that love is not a noun but a verb—a call to action.

Powhatan, Deloria, hooks, Gatensby, and the community in São Pedro Village all illustrate how to follow this road map for making strangers relatives and centering love. They bring hope that Indigenous Peoples and settlers can become relatives to one another and act in love to effectively address harms and wrongdoings, including those that affect the Natural World. Humans, like all living beings, are engaged in life-transforming processes, growing and transforming day by day, just like how a seed becomes an apple. The next chapter explores how to integrate these ideas into a multidimensional restorative justice approach to address settler-related environmental injustice and harm.

Chapter 6
Multidimensional Restorative Justice

Restorative justice is not a map, but the principles of restorative justice can be seen as a compass offering direction.[1]

—Howard Zehr

The idea of making strangers relatives orients us to handle settler-related environmental issues restoratively, in a way that builds relationships and engages with the world through love and non-harm. While conventional restorative justice practices—such as peacemaking circles, discussed in the previous chapter—can be valuable tools for gathering people and resolving harmful conflicts, they may not always be sufficient when addressing complex issues like environmental harm and injustice and their ties to settler colonialism, especially if used without an expanded vision of the problem at hand.

Just as Howard Zehr suggests that we need to change the lenses through which we perceive justice and wrongdoing,[2] we also need to broaden our restorative lenses to address environmental injustice and harm. To achieve this, we must adjust our perspective to a multidimensional framework that includes individuals and groups whose relationships have been disrupted or broken due to colonization, thus resulting in changes that harm both human and other-than-human beings.

This chapter explores such an approach. We call it "multidimensional restorative justice." We begin by sharing the story of an Indigenous People in Brazil, the Guarani Kaiowa, who have suffered greatly due to the settlers' presence in their homeland and from whom we can learn lessons about a multidimensional framework. We then outline what a multidimensional restorative justice perspective entails, inspired by Alberto Guerreiro Ramos's concept of multidimensionality. This theoretical framework provides the foundation for the fourteen points we present next, aimed at restoring settler environmental harm and injustice. We close with a discussion of a multifocal lens connected to the approach presented before.

Guarani Kaiowa's Land Reclamation

This land reclamation case occurred in Mato Grosso do Sul, a Brazilian state notably affected by settler colonialism throughout the twentieth and twenty-first centuries. In 2024, the Commission for Land Solutions (CLS) of the Federal Court of Justice was asked to intervene in various conflicts involving ranchers and the Guarani Kaiowa, a Native People who have lived in the region since time immemorial.

Previously, in the mid-twentieth century, federal and state governments facilitated settlers' acquisition of private properties on land that was originally Indigenous. Their goal was development, specifically to establish settlements and pursue agribusiness. This led to the forced removal of the Guarani Kaiowa from their homeland. Many violent tactics were employed—such as deception, murder, threats, assault, hanging, co-optation, cultural assimilation, and Christianization—to achieve this removal. Some Indigenous people migrated to neighboring Paraguay, while others remained in Brazil near their original territory without having their lands recognized or protected.

The settlers' agribusiness in the Guarani Kaiowa's homeland transformed its natural landscape and resulted in poverty and starvation. After enduring these difficult conditions for years, the Guarani Kaiowa decided to reclaim parts of their land through a strategy in which they reoccupied areas that settlers claimed as private property. This led to several violent confrontations, some directly with ranchers and others with the police. Some clashes resulted in physical assaults, arrests, and even the deaths of Indigenous people. Despite the violence settlers perpetrated against the Guarani Kaiowa, they have not abandoned the strategy of reclaiming their traditional lands.

Some of these land claim cases have been referred to the CLS, which has begun conducting dialogues to address the issue. These dialogues have revealed the complexity of the conflict between the Guarani Kaiowa and the settlers. They indicated that the conflict arose from political decisions that enabled settlers to "develop" lands traditionally inhabited by Indigenous Peoples. They revealed that the Guarani Kaiowa's resurgence on their stolen land significantly affected the settlers' businesses and threatened their private property titles. Other landowners feared similar consequences since the entire region constitutes unceded Indigenous land, especially since other Indigenous groups in Brazil adopted the Guarani Kaiowa strategy of reoccupying land.

In reaction to this growing trend, Brazil's National Congress proposed the "Time Frame Thesis" law stating that only the lands Indigenous Peoples occupied before 1988, the year Brazil ratified its constitution, would be recognized as legally Indigenous lands. However, shortly before the National Congress approved the law, the Supreme Court of Brazil declared it unconstitutional. As a result, CLS realized that the dispute between the Guarani Kaiowa and settlers was situated within a broader legal, constitutional, and political discussion and could not be resolved solely by addressing the specific conflicts involving the Indigenous communities of Mato Grosso do Sul.

To address such a complex situation, the CLS gathered various stakeholders to negotiate solutions to the conflicts. In all cases, meeting participants included the Guarani Kaiowa and ranchers as well as representatives from the Ministry of Indigenous Peoples, the Ministry of Agrarian Development, the National Foundation of Indigenous Peoples, the state government, and the prosecutor's office. In some instances, representatives from the National Council of Justice also aided the CLS. In another case, the Brazilian Supreme Court Justice Gilmar Mendes took part in the negotiations, facilitating the construction of an agreement. Regardless, given the complexities involved, these multilateral discussions disclosed that resolution of these cases would have been impossible without a multidimensional approach.

The outcomes of the dialogues among the participants varied due to the uniqueness of each case and thus could not be approached in the same manner. For instance, in the case where a Supreme Court Justice intervened, the Brazilian state had recognized Indigenous land a decade before the negotiations. In this situation, where the police murdered an Indigenous person, Neri Guarani Kaiowa, on the Indigenous land known as Ñande Ru Marangatu, an agreement was reached stating that the federal and state governments would compensate the ranchers if they vacated the land immediately.

In another case, the landback process, through which lands are returned to Indigenous Peoples, had already officially begun but was later taken to court because the ranchers claimed the right to remain on the land and continue their production. After the CLS's intervention and some multilateral dialogues, the ranchers agreed to negotiate with the Brazilian government about purchasing their properties. If crops could not be harvested during the season, they would also receive financial compensation for lost profits. In a third case, it was recognized that an Indigenous land acknowledgment and landback process were necessary but required action from the National Foundation of Indigenous Peoples that had not yet been taken. When we finished writing this book, the process had not yet started.

A key aspect of the Guarani Kaiowa case is the relationship with the Natural World. The settlers' forced occupation of Guarani Kaiowa lands has not only harmed an Indigenous homeland but also resulted in its ecological change. The lands have been commodified, turned into private property, and converted into pastures and agricultural fields. Furthermore, the other-than-human beings who inhabit these lands are no longer regarded as peoples with whom humans should maintain a respectful relationship. Consequently, the concept of good living—*teko porã* in the Guarani language—has been severely disrupted. The Indigenous strategy for reclaiming their traditional lands aims to restore these vital relationships with the Natural World and heal the harm that settlers inflicted.

A Multidimensional Restorative Justice Framework

The reclamation of Guarani Kaiowa land is a powerful example of what a multidimensional restorative justice framework involves. To deepen our understanding of this framework, this section reviews the one-dimensional settler mindset and presents an alternative to it, followed by fourteen points for implementing multidimensional restorative justice to address environmental harm and injustice related to settler colonialism.

Settlers' One-Dimensional Mindset

The Guarani Kaiowa story illustrates how settlers, fixated on the market, imposed a one-dimensional mindset onto Indigenous homelands. This mindset gave rise to concepts like land development and privatization in Abya Yala. However, this mentality legitimizes the violence inflicted on Indigenous Peoples and the Natural World and views it as normal, expected, customary, and even necessary—and always justified either using the "Doctrine of Discovery" or the demands of development.

Even when settlers attempt to remedy environmental harm and injustice, their emphasis remains mainly on economic responses, such as financial compensation, carbon pricing, green investment and financing, subsidies and incentives for restoration, payment for ecosystem services, pollution taxes and environmental levies, and so on. These responses neither hold wrongdoers responsible nor dismantle ongoing settler structures. They fail to prevent future violations from occurring repeatedly and without restraint. Given this, a multidimensional framework for restorative justice is needed.

Our understanding of multidimensionality draws on *The New Science of Organizations: A Reconceptualization of the Wealth of Nations* by the late Alberto Guerreiro Ramos. This Afro-Brazilian sociologist argues that human life has been reduced to mere economic value in a society driven by the mass market. He criticizes the pursuit of an unrestricted economy, noting that this "limitless" economic model forms the foundation of contemporary settler societies. The mass market–driven societal mindset overlooks vital aspects of human existence, such as our deep connection with all our Natural World relatives. Thus, it fails to embrace multidimensionality and limits opportunities for a good life. As has been argued throughout the book, this non-multidimensional perspective has led to social injustice and racism, genocide and ethnic cleansing, climate change, and significant human-induced ecological destruction in Abya Yala.

Multidimensional Orientation to Heal Environmental Harm and Injustice

An alternative to this one-dimensional settler mindset is to think, communicate, and act in multidimensional ways, returning to Indigenous Peoples' ways of being. This approach can help us better comprehend and tackle environmental injustice and harm by transcending a mentality primarily focusing on economic concerns. It steers us toward a more holistic view of human life by creating space and time for multiple dimensions of our existence—interconnected with other-than-human beings.

Inspired by Indigenous teachings of Abya Yala—such as the Medicine Wheel and other symbols shared by Native Peoples—we visually represent the holistic vision inherent in multidimensionality, when applied to addressing environmental harm and injustice, as

a wheel. This wheel includes the psychological, relational, social, cultural, political, economic, ecological, and spiritual dimensions—each of which must be considered when addressing settler-related environmental issues. There are likely other dimensions that may be important in certain cases, though they are not included in this wheel.

A multidimensional perspective recognizes that settler environmental harm and injustice are not solely linked to the *ecological* changes driven by *economic* activities. These harms can inflict lasting psychological trauma on the individuals and communities affected. They involve *relationships*—such as those between Indigenous Peoples and settlers, between White people, Black people, and other People of Color, and between humans and other-than-human relatives. Harms are also closely tied to *social* injustices and *cultural* clashes, particularly the encounters and tensions between settler and Indigenous worldviews. They are rooted in *political* decisions. Environmental harms and injustices affect the *spiritual* dimension of life, as they disrupt sacred places and even the broader cosmological order.

With this multidimensional consciousness, we look beyond merely seeking pragmatic solutions to environmental conflicts because reaching agreements to address immediate problems only tackles part of the problem but not the entire issue. For example, it is not enough to provide financial restitution as compensation for stolen lands and environmental damage without addressing Native Peoples' long-overdue demands for justice and protection for cherished relatives from the Natural World. Effective responses need to consider other foundational concerns. Katerina Friesen, a Christian pastor and organizer with the Coalition to Dismantle the Doctrine of Discovery, refers to this type of response:

> a spectrum of actions on the part of settlers and Christians that seek—to the fullest extent possible—to repair harms done to Indigenous Peoples as a result of the Doctrine of Discovery, to end ongoing harm, and to restore Indigenous sovereignty and lands. . . . These actions should be responsive to the context and needs of Indigenous groups, and may include solidarity actions, land return, financial restitution, and advocacy for just laws and policies.[3]

According to the approach presented here, these responses should focus on good living, being good relatives, and restorative justice cornerstones of identifying those who are being or have been harmed, repairing past and ongoing damages, preventing current harms, and avoiding future harms through proactive measures. The usual economy-based responses can still be activated, though they become less important.

How can we come together to heal the wounds settler colonialism inflicted? We outline fourteen points inspired by the continuing calls for justice from Indigenous Peoples.

1: Embracing a Multigenerational Perspective
In Abya Yala, both North and South, we confidently assert that contemporary environmental injustice and harm stem from the First Harm and the persistence of settlers' illegal occupation of Indigenous lands. As

such, we are confronting a multigenerational problem: one that looks to the distant past to understand how The First Harm originated, manifests in the present, and is transmitted to the future. This look includes harm to humans and extends to their relative, the Natural World, as seen in the cases of the Buffalo, the Water, and the Black Hills in the Oyáte's homeland. Adopting a multigenerational perspective is crucial for healing today's environmental wounds and preventing harm from being passed on to future generations.

2: Truth-Telling
Healing will never occur if the truth is silenced or ignored. While climate change has played a crucial role in raising our awareness of environmental concerns, it has not been enough to transform the persistent reality of settler colonialism or the carnage the Doctrine of Discovery has caused since 1492. The time has come for everyone to confront the profound trauma that settlers' invasions and the forced seizure of Indigenous lands have caused to Indigenous Peoples and the Natural World. Embracing the truth means acknowledging that settlers (white and otherwise) continue to unlawfully occupy Indigenous lands and refuse to return them.

Like all truths, acknowledging and reckoning with the wrongs committed by our settler ancestors is never easy and is always painful. Nevertheless, it is the primary challenge many of us face due to the ongoing nature of the First Harm. As settlers still perceive the theft of Indigenous land as a virtue, this mindset creates emotional discomfort around returning stolen lands or protecting those that remain untouched. Yet, this act can also be liberating. It can free us from the burden of guilt and shame, as well as from the continuation of injustice resulting from the First Harm.

3: Taking Responsibility

The next step is to take responsibility. For many settlers, it may seem that any responsibility for colonial violence, including environmental harms, belongs to their ancestors rather than to themselves or current generations. However, the wealth that today's settlers have acquired is ill-gotten across generations, stemming from the First Harm.

A formal apology is one way to externalize that we take responsibility for the harm caused, but it should not be the sole response. Apologies alone do not and have not stopped advances into Indigenous lands nor transformed the frontier mindset. Some governments and institutions have issued sincere apologies, paired with actionable commitments to address past and present harms inflicted by settlers. For example, Canada established a Truth and Reconciliation Commission (TRC) to document settler violence, cultural erasure, and land dispossession. Churches responsible for Canadian residential schools have also publicly apologized for the damage they inflicted. The TRC issued ninety-four calls to action designed to address the enduring impacts of residential schools and promote reconciliation between Indigenous Peoples and settlers. These calls to action span various areas, including child welfare, education, health, language, justice, and the role of churches in repairing harms.

4: Repairing Harms

For restorative justice to be genuinely achieved, harm can never be left unaddressed. While harm repair may include economy-based responses, they are insufficient. For example, in *United States v. Sioux Nation of Indians* (1980), the settlers' Supreme Court offered the Oyáte financial restitution for the "taking" of their homeland. The Oyáte rejected any monetary settlement and demanded the return of their stolen land. Their homeland is sacred, and their land is not for sale.

The Oyaté's refusal to accept money for their land does not rule out other forms of reparation, such as compensation for forced assimilation policies, investments in infrastructure, health care, and housing in Indigenous communities, and support for Indigenous enterprises through grants, tax incentives, and equitable partnerships. We could also tackle systemic barriers in employment and education, engage in public education campaigns, revise school curricula to include Indigenous worldviews, and support Indigenous colleges and universities. Regardless of the path we take, it is crucial to listen to those who have been harmed and obtain their sovereign consent. It is about consulting Indigenous Peoples on how they perceive repair and actively involving them in all processes related to achieving reparation.

5: Respecting Sovereignty and Self-Determination

Indigenous Peoples are the original inhabitants of Abya Yala and have an inherent right to exist peacefully as sovereign nations. The continents known as "The Americas" are, in reality, comprised of plurinational states, including the United States and Brazil.

Native Peoples possess inherent sovereignty within these states and have a national status tied to self-determination. They view their relationship with settler states as nation-to-nation.

In response to Indigenous demands for sovereignty, a few settler states, like Ecuador and Bolivia, have officially recognized their multinational nature, consisting of both Indigenous and non-Indigenous nations that must coexist harmoniously. The constitutions of these multinational states have incorporated the Indigenous-inspired term "good living" to reflect their citizens' commitment to living as "good relatives."

However, the majority of settler states still do not fully recognize this, even when they acknowledge that Indigenous Peoples have the right to self-determination. To enforce Indigenous sovereignty and self-determination, settler states must, at the very least, protect Indigenous lands from further theft and nonconsensual actions and return lands that are culturally significant and vital for the sustainability of Indigenous Peoples' livelihoods.

6: *Getting Prior, Free, and Informed Consent*

Healing environmental harm and injustice necessitates that Indigenous voices and the Natural World (or, in settler terms, primary stakeholders) are genuinely heard. Being heard goes beyond merely checking the "duty-to-consult" box with Native Peoples and pretending that due diligence has been met.

For Indigenous Peoples, being heard means obtaining their sovereign consent through prior, free, and informed measures. Indigenous Peoples have the right to be consulted before any action affecting their lives and lands. This consent must be obtained freely, without pressure, manipulation, or co-optation, while respecting Indigenous decision-making processes. It is essential to act without tokenism, ensuring all affected Peoples are recognized in ways that align with their own practices. Some Indigenous communities have established protocols outlining how consultation should take place. Information must be clear, accessible to the general public, and translated into Native languages. Anything less than securing consent in this way inflicts harm and perpetuates violence.

7: Acknowledging Indigenous Land
In recent years, it has become common in settler societies to read Indigenous Land Acknowledgments (ILA) aloud. These verbal or written statements aim to raise awareness and confront the audience about the illegal occupation of Indigenous lands, ill-gotten wealth, and the intergenerational transfer of that wealth. This unsettling reality sometimes prompts the audience to reflect and seek appropriate ways to address the past and present harms.

While these declarations are an important step in truth-telling and acknowledging responsibility, they are often performative and do not change the reality that Indigenous lands were taken through settler violence and coercion, nor do they address the ongoing illegal seizure of Indigenous lands today. Words alone are not enough to prevent, stop, undo, or repair the damage. Actions are needed.

A better, restorative justice–inspired ILA could outline the following: which lands were stolen, who the affected Indigenous Peoples are, who the wrongdoers are, the impacts on People, relationships, and the Natural World, who can aid in repairing the harms, and the actions we can take to prevent further harm—such as returning stolen land and safeguarding Indigenous lands.

8: Returning Stolen Land and Keeping Safe the Untouched Ones

From Indigenous Peoples' perspective, there is little choice settlers have but to return the lands stolen from them and keep the untouched Indigenous territories safe. This act is essential to halting the ongoing genocide against Native Peoples in Abya Yala, both North and South. It also requires demonstrating to the world that Indigenous lives matter and that Indigenous territories deserve the same respect as those of any other nation.

One approach to stop both overt and subtle encroachments on Indigenous lands is to have a strong legal framework that explicitly recognizes and protects these territories. This approach involves governments ratifying and enforcing the original United Nations Declaration on the Rights of Indigenous Peoples (UNDRIP). The original UNDRIP was weakened to favor settler states by restricting Indigenous Peoples' access to international forums. Indigenous groups that have become aware of the original version of UNDRIP reject the approved version and seek the original, which better protects their rights. Efforts are underway to push for its recognition, as states, institutions, and allies are not mandated to accept the diluted approved version. Settler states prefer the approved UNDRIP because it allows them to maintain control and evade accountability.

Regardless of which version is taken, as the Standing Rock case (Chapter 3) illustrated, even with legal protections in place, settlers often covet Indigenous lands. Thus, changing settler behaviors is crucial, not just enacting laws.

9: Revitalizing Indigenous Cultures

Revitalizing Indigenous cultures encompasses, but is not limited to, languages, ceremonies, cosmologies, mythologies, philosophies, sciences, arts, and traditional ecological knowledge. For over five centuries, colonizers systematically persecuted and prosecuted Indigenous Peoples for practicing their own cultures. The case of the "Good Fire" (Chapter 4) stands as one example out of tens of thousands.

One way to do this is to support Indigenous language programs, cultural centers, and oral history projects that revitalize Indigenous cultures. Efforts can focus on protecting sacred sites and safeguarding intellectual property from unauthorized use or appropriation. Decolonizing institutions is also critical. Museums and universities, for instance, should prioritize repatriating culturally significant artifacts and collaborating with Indigenous communities on curation and research. Moreover, centering Indigenous leadership in environmental policy, respecting traditional ecological knowledge, and legally recognizing Native environmental stewardship practices can significantly impact the protection of the Natural World.

10: Protecting the Natural World

Healing environmental harm and injustice requires a perspective that encompasses and protects other-than-human living beings, which goes hand in hand with respect for Indigenous Peoples and their lands. For centuries, Indigenous Peoples have played a central role in environmental conservation, working harmoniously with our Natural World relatives, despite the ongoing encroachment of settlers into their homelands.

While we acknowledge that settlers' environmental efforts have contributed significantly to protecting the environment, they remain limited because they are deeply rooted in an anthropocentric view (usually market-driven) of the relationship between humans and the Natural World.

There are many other ways of relating to the environment that could be taught and learned to restore harmony and good living in Abya Yala. For instance, we could teach the Oyáte worldview that engages other-than-humans as relatives. In this view, all living things possess inherent dignity and a right to coexist alongside their human counterparts. Many Indigenous Peoples in Abya Yala share this or a similar view.

11: Restoring Moral Relations

One of the most challenging steps is repairing the moral relationships among human beings and the Natural World. The good news is that many non-Indigenous people have already shown a willingness to engage, as seen through their various waves of environmentalism.

However, despite progress in this area, we now face environmental denialism—a refusal by some to fully acknowledge the extent of the damage settler colonialism has caused to the Natural World and Indigenous lands. This denial can take many forms, such as dismissing or minimizing the seriousness of environmental issues. As a result, we encounter both progress and setbacks in environmental policies. This moral instability surrounding the environment reflects the unpredictability of strangers, especially settlers (see Chapter 5).

The Oyáte's approach to relationality—transforming strangers into relatives and becoming good kin—could be a bold step forward in restoring moral relations in Abya Yala. It has the potential to constructively reshape our relationships with other-than-humans. But this will only happen if settlers are genuinely willing to become good relatives.

12: Addressing Social Injustice

A multidimensional approach connects social issues with the Natural World. It seeks to transform the underlying factors that contribute to environmental injustice and facilitate harm, to the fullest extent possible. Neglecting these issues makes creating positive, sustainable long-term solutions challenging.

We cannot ignore that inequity, exclusion, racism, ethnocentrism, classism, xenophobia, poverty, and other forms of social injustice are deeply intertwined with environmental degradation. The harms and risks of settler development have primarily impacted Indigenous Peoples, Black individuals, and other People of Color, as well as the impoverished and working class, while white settlers largely reap the benefits. This assessment may be an inconvenient truth, but the Natural World and all colonized Peoples are calling—if not screaming—for settlers to take responsibility for the social harm their actions have caused.

13: Strengthening Community

In addressing environmental injustice and harm, strengthening community is essential. The distress and pressures caused by harmful settler activities often lead to community fragmentation and a weakened sense of solidarity. Certain businesses and even the government exploit these divisions to expand their interests and consolidate power over the affected people and groups. To achieve their goals, they often co-opt community leaders, encouraging them to act based on personal gain rather than the vision of good living. In his influential work *Pedagogy of the Oppressed*,[4] the Brazilian philosopher and educator Paulo Freire describes this strategy as "divide and rule."

A crucial step in countering this approach is to apply restorative justice practices, such as circles, to rebuild unity, foster dialogue, and restore values within communities. These efforts should empower community members through training them in how to conduct peacemaking circles and other restorative justice activities, addressing the enduring structures that negatively impact "all our relatives," both human and other-than-human.

14: Engaging in Multilateral Dialogues

Due to the complexity of environmental cases, a restorative justice approach requires the involvement of multiple actors and levels of power to generate visionary, creative responses. Such intricate cases often require a multilateral dialogue model rather than meetings with only those directly involved in the conflict. As illustrated in the conflict between the Guarani Kaiowa and settlers, decades-old open wounds are tied to the government-facilitated forced seizure of Indigenous lands. Consequently, engaging federal and state governmental departments, various branches of the judiciary, and the prosecutor's office has been crucial. In some instances, universities and civil society organizations can support or facilitate the dialogue and negotiation process.

Furthermore, a multidisciplinary team is often essential for conducting studies and research, providing the necessary information for informed decision-making. This work helps analyze the conflict by examining the social, economic, political, cultural, and even spiritual dimensions of the issue, among other factors. Occasionally, multidisciplinary work may be necessary to identify the individuals and groups affected, assess the damage and risks they have incurred, and, to develop effective responses collectively, assist participants in multilateral dialogues to gather the most secure and accurate information.

Multifocal Lens

As highlighted throughout this book, responding to and repairing settler environmental harm and injustice has a long-term timeline requiring a multifocal lens oriented toward the past, present, and future. It is necessary to consider all points along this timeline to effectively address settler-related environmental problems.

The diagram below visually depicts this multifocal lens with past, present, and future axes. At its center are a current environmental issue, with various harms, dimensions, people, and actions needing attention extending along each axis.

Multidimensional Restorative Justice

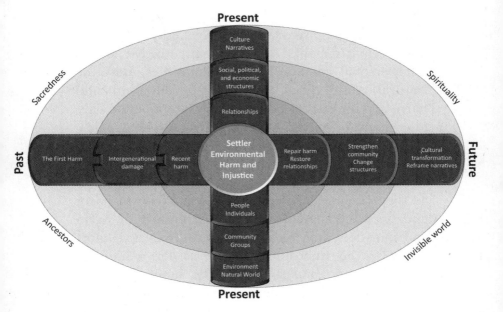

Past

The axis of the past shows that environmental issues often began but did not simply "rest in peace" with the First Harm. Since this harm remained unhealed and was passed down through generations, it became structural and manifests today as ongoing harm to Indigenous Peoples and the Natural World. Even when people are aware of the First Harm, many, especially settlers, tend to silence it or take a denialist stance that avoids confronting the root causes of contemporary environmental issues. Thus, settler colonialism remains an underlying structure at the core of environmental and other conflicts we face today and looking to and repairing the past is essential.

Present

The axis of the present emphasizes that any contemporary environmental issues typically involve people, interpersonal relationships, communities, and the Natural World. Thus, responding to environmental harm and injustice necessitates our attention not only to ecological dimension but also to the relationships, structures, cultural factors, and narratives at play.

For example, social, economic, and political dimensions of an environmental issue must be addressed as they become structures that contribute to harm and violence. Furthermore, environmental harm and injustice often have a cultural dimension, most critically the imposition of the settler worldview on Indigenous Peoples. Hence, the suppression and persecution of Indigenous languages and cultural practices, Christianization, the disregard for traditional ecological knowledge, and the undermining of Indigenous environmental stewardship must be addressed. Finally, current environmental problems are deeply lodged in Doctrine of Discovery narratives and are invisibly embedded in land development discourses. Knowledge of these narratives and how they function is essential to addressing environmental issues in Abya Yala. What we do with this knowledge belongs in the future axis.

Future

In the future axis, we envision responses to environmental harm and injustice that unfold in the immediate, medium, and long term. The immediate term emphasizes relationality with the focus on repairing recent harm and restoring relationships, particularly for those directly affected and including the Natural World.

In the medium term, it becomes crucial to strengthen communities and support affected groups in recovering from the traumagenic events and structures that often lead to internal divisions and conflicts. Additionally, to prevent the recurrence of violence and promote good living, it is necessary to dismantle the oppressive structures that underpin violations against people and relationships. One way to achieve this is by developing policies supporting community self-determination in which individuals and groups have control of their futures.

In the long term, cultural transformation and the reframing of narratives are essential. This entails revitalizing Indigenous cultures and transforming the Western anthropocentric perspectives to support a holistic view that does not divide humanity from Nature and does not subscribe to the belief in human superiority within the cosmological order. This alternative way, aiming for a multicultural world, transcends the one-dimensional, market-driven settler mindset. To achieve this, however, it is vital to dismantle colonial narratives that marginalize Indigenous Peoples and their cultures. These narratives justified the ongoing theft of Indigenous lands, environmental degradation, the violation of our cherished Natural World relatives, and the suppression or at least devaluation of Native worldviews.

What the Eyes Don't See

The diagram also reveals aspects of human experience that the typical lens overlooks—the spiritual dimension of human existence and, by extension, environmental issues. For Indigenous Peoples, the visible world is continuously interconnected with the invisible realm. Because sacredness permeates all things, environmental damage and injustice is a violation of sacred people and spaces. The conflicts arising from settler colonialism are deeply woven into our shared history—both settler and Indigenous—entangled with the actions and legacies of our ancestors, whether on one side or the other. Therefore, healing settler harm, including to the Natural World, is inherently a spiritual matter. In this process, we can seek the support of spiritual leaders, such as shamans and healers, who can lead ceremonies and facilitate dialogues between the visible and invisible worlds, helping us better understand and address environmental issues. While this may seem unfamiliar to many people, it is crucial to Indigenous Peoples' understanding of environmental challenges.

As illustrated in the multifocal lens diagram, all these multiple foci are interconnected, meaning that addressing one requires consideration of the others. Therefore, healing settler-led harms and addressing environmental injustice present inherently complex tasks that require a multidimensional approach.

A Compass, Not a Map

A multidimensional restorative justice approach may seem overwhelming for those accustomed to responding to situations that have been reduced to a few manageable issues and one-dimensional thinking. This simplification in complex restorative justice cases only distorts reality. Though complex, multidimensional restorative justice does not need to be complicated. Practical tools for such an approach are underway though they remain a work in progress. As the quote from Professor Zehr, which started this chapter, states, restorative justice is a compass, not a map. It indicates a direction rather than a means to reach a destination. The same can be said for multidimensional restorative justice. It guides us toward meaningfully healing settler harms and addressing environmental injustice. Given this, we recognize that we are fledglings learning to fly—and we have little choice but to attempt to fly. But there is hope because we do not have to fly alone.

Chapter 7
The Eagle and the Condor

Among several Indigenous Peoples, a prophecy states that the Sun and the Moon created the Eagle and the Condor. However, one day, the Eagle overpowered the Condor, creating an imbalance on Earth. The prophecy tells that the Eagle and the Condor will fly together again, restoring a much-needed balance on the planet. Naturally, there are many interpretations of this ancient story. One interpretation suggests that the Eagle represents the settlers while the Condor symbolizes the Indigenous Peoples. Another version emphasizes that the Eagle is far-seeing, rational, linear, and one-dimensional in vision, while the Condor embodies a connection to Earth, wisdom, intuition, and holistic perception. Yet another view posits that the Eagle represents Indigenous Peoples from the North and the Condor symbolizes Indigenous Peoples from the South. Ultimately, some versions merge elements of these interpretations, teaching that a day will come when peoples from the four directions gather to restore balance. At that moment, Indigenous wisdom will be added to the settlers' knowledge; the farsighted will meet the land-connected, rationality will encounter spirituality, linearity will encounter diversity, and science will know sacred tradition.

Regardless of interpretation, the joint flights of the Eagle and the Condor serve as a powerful metaphor for restorative and environmental justice aimed at halting ecological harm. This prophecy, now a prediction, has been referenced to discuss the collaborative efforts observed today in addressing climate change and the harmful disconnection—failing to act as good relatives—taking place on the planet. It can be difficult to imagine solutions that involve dialogues between settlers and Indigenous Peoples and between settlers and the Natural World.

Nonetheless, as we enter the third decade of the twenty-first century, we have become increasingly aware of the emergence of the Anthropocene, a new geological age defined by human influence and climate change. So, it is impossible to think about the sustainability of life on Earth without the collective effort of diverse peoples coming together from all directions and working out ways to be good relatives. We are unlikely to discover solutions to contemporary dilemmas without dialogic processes and perspectives incorporating the multiple dimensions of caring for (Grand)Mother Earth. Therefore, there is an urgency for the Eagle and the Condor to return (or finally begin) to fly together, as Indigenous Peoples predicted.

Let us revisit an example from the first chapter of this book: the flood in Rio Grande do Sul. This Brazilian state is the homeland of several Indigenous Peoples—including the Kaingang, Guarani, Charrua, and Xokleng—whose lands were forcibly taken by settlers. Despite the historical suffering endured by their ancestors, the wisdom of Indigenous Peoples has been utilized to help heal the trauma experienced by countless individuals and families affected by the flood, many of whom were settlers. The Carcross/Tagish First Nation, particularly brothers Harold and Phillip Gatensby, introduced peacemaking circles to Canadian Judge Barry Stuart. Through Kay Pranis, a white American settler and restorative justice practitioner mentioned earlier, these circles found their way to Brazil. Thanks to the efforts of many volunteer circle keepers, most of whom Pranis and her students trained, restorative justice provided emotional support to hundreds, possibly thousands, of victims of this climate change–related environmental disaster. Despite the violence of Brazil's settlers, Indigenous Peoples, like Powhatan, extended their love to them. However, Brazilian settlers willingly embraced this love, unlike those who rejected Powhatan's offer in 1609. We hope that settlers will return such love in kind.

    This little book aims to show that restorative justice is a path to address contemporary environmental issues. We, the authors, are both settlers and Indigenous peoples, speaking from different locales, places, and languages. Our life experiences are contradictory, and our worldviews are not identical. We encountered numerous challenges and obstacles along our journey. However, despite the distances that separate us, we combined our minds, hearts, and hands to write about a complex and uncomfortable topic. While we had few in-person meetings to accomplish this, virtual spaces enabled us to navigate this challenging task. We sought to bring our realities closer, get to know each other—and, yes, make strangers into relatives—and build good relationships as much as possible. We did not always see eye to eye on every issue, but we dedicated ourselves to addressing our differences and devising solutions based on our diversity. Perhaps not everything turned out perfectly. We believe we experienced a bit of the Eagle's and the Condor's dilemma, which is unlikely to ever be completely resolved. It was challenging, but we flew together as best we could.

Finally, we honor all environmental protectors and land defenders, whether they are settlers or Indigenous Peoples. Sometimes their efforts clash because of opposing worldviews. However, all efforts to protect and defend the Natural World should be seen as a way to restore the kinship that humans have disregarded with our other-than-human relatives. Much like a circle that does not elevate hierarchy, we must also sit upon the land (Grandmother's robe) to communicate and engage in horizontal conversations. Settler environmentalism must be receptive to Indigenous Peoples, and vice versa. We feel this mutual exchange will indeed create new possibilities. The dialogue among the various schools of environmentalism is also a meeting of the Eagle with the Condor, a form of collaborative flight in search of good relational living.

This little book invites you to join this collective journey, whether you are a settler or from Indigenous Peoples. Restorative justice exists not only as an effort to work alongside environmental justice to heal the wounds that settler colonialism has inflicted in its storied history. More crucially, individuals who are strangers to one another and to the Natural World have a chance to transform themselves into All My Relatives.

Resources

Readings
Restorative Justice
- Elizabeth Elliott. *Security with Care: Restorative Justice and Healthy Societies.* Nova Scotia: Fernwood Publishing, 2011.
- Howard Zehr. *Changing Lenses: Restorative Justice for Our Times.* Harrisonburg; Kitchener: Herald Press, 2015.
- Howard Zehr, Lorraine Stutzman Amstutz, Allan MacRae, and Kay Pranis. *The Big Book of Restorative Justice.* New York: Good Books, 2015.

Environment and Restorative Justice
- Ben Almassi. *Reparative Environmental Justice in a World of Wounds.* Lanham, MD: Lexington Books, 2021.
- Brunilda Pali et al. (editors). *The Palgrave Handbook of Environmental Restorative Justice.* London: Palgrave Macmillan, 2022.
- Carla Zamith Boin Aguiar, João Salm, and Katia Herminia Martins Lazarano Roncada (editors). *Restorative Justice and the Environment.* Brazil: AJUFE, 2022.

Indigenous Ways of Justice
- Rupert Ross. *Return to Teaching: Exploring Aboriginal Justice*. Toronto: Penguin, 1996.
- Wanda D. McCaslin (editor). *Justice as Healing: Indigenous Ways*. Saint Paul: Living Justice Press, 2005.

Environmental Justice and Indigenous Worldviews
- Dina Gilio-Whitaker. *As Long as Grass Grows: The Indigenous Fight for Environmental Justice, from Colonization to Standing Rock*. Boston: Beacon Press, 2019.
- Nick Estes and Jaskiran Dhillon. *Standing with Standing Rock: Voices from the #NoDAPL Movement*. Minneapolis: University of Minnesota Press, 2019.

Traditional Ecological Knowledge
- Kari Marie Norgaard. *Karuk Traditional Ecological Knowledge and the Need for Knowledge Sovereignty: Social, Cultural and Economic Impacts of Denied Access to Traditional Management*. Orleans: Karuk Tribe Department of Natural Resources, 2014.
- Melissa K. Nelson and Dan Shilling (editors). *Traditional Ecological Knowledge: Learning from Indigenous Practices for Environmental Sustainability*. Cambridge and New York: Cambridge University Press, 2018.

Settler Colonialism
- Edward Charles Valandra. "Undoing the First Harm: Settlers in Restorative Justice," in *Colorizing Restorative Justice: Voicing our Realities*. Saint Paul: Living Justice Press, 2020.
- Eve Tuck and K. Wayne Yang. "Decolonization Is Not a Metaphor." *Decolonization: Indigeneity, Education & Society* 1, no. 1 (2012).
- Patrick Wolfe. "Settler Colonialism and the Elimination of the Native." *Journal of Genocide Research* 8, no. 4 (2006).
- Waziyatawin. *What Does Justice Look Like? The Struggle for Liberation in Dakota Homeland*. Saint Paul: Living Justice Press, 2008.

Documentaries
Canada and US Context
- *YINTAH: A Decade of Wet'suwet'en Resistance* (2024).
- *In the Light of Reverence* (2001).
- *Denying Access: NODAPL to NODAPL* (2020).
- *Inhabitants: Indigenous Perspectives on Restoring Our World* (2021).

Brazil Context
- *The Last Forest* (2021).
- *The Territory* (2022).
- *The Falling Sky* (2024).

Webinar

- Kay Pranis and Samuel Johann. *Using Circles to Support Individual and Community Mental Health in a Climate Disaster.* Harrisonburg: Zehr Institute for Restorative Justice, 2025.

Podcast

- Claire de Mezerville López, Brunilda Pali, and Nirson Medeiros da Silva Neto. "Restorative Justice in the Amazon: Communities, Nature, and Conflict." *Restorative Works!* International Institute for Restorative Practices and European Forum for Restorative Justice, 2024.

Acknowledgments

Writing this little book on environment and restorative justice would not have been possible without the collaboration of many people and institutions that were part of the personal and professional trajectory of each of the authors, whose names we will not be able to mention because doing so would fill many pages. Some, however, made an important contribution to the publication of this book.

Governors State University in Chicago's Southland (GSU) supported the project by inviting Nirson Neto in 2021 for a one-year stint as a research scholar, which provided the beginning of the research and writing work on the first draft. Among our colleagues at this university, we express gratitude to Cheryl Green (in memory), then president of GSU, who passed away shortly before this book was published, and to Ben Almassi for the fruitful conversations on the subject of the book and for clarifying key issues of environmentalism in the United States.

Likewise, we express our gratitude to our colleagues at Eastern Mennonite University (EMU), especially to Professor Vernon Jantzi, who encouraged us to continue with the project at critical moments when we thought it would not be possible—they pointed the way and helped us overcome the obstacles that presented themselves in these hours of uncertainty about the feasibility of the project.

Some of the stories told directly relate to the struggles of the Indigenous Peoples of the Abya Yala, both North and South. We owe special recognition to the Očhéthi Šakówiŋ Oyáte, to which Waŋblí Wapȟáha Hokšíla belongs, as well as our friends from the Tapajós-Arapiuns Indigenous Council, from whom we learned a lot about what restorative justice means for Native Peoples and how to experience it in the face of conflicts involving environmental issues.

We thank Chief justice Robert Yazzie and Peterson Zah (in memory) from the Navajo Nation; both provided knowledge and were the first to teach João Salm about restorative justice. We deeply thank Professor Elizabeth Elliott (in memory), who passed on her knowledge of restorative justice to him.

Brazilian Judge Isabel Maria Sampaio Oliveira Lima played a crucial role in connecting Josineide and Nirson to the broader restorative justice movement, both nationally and internationally. She was the first to highlight their responsibility to bring discussions about restorative justice and the environment into focus. On her behalf, we thank all the judges who have been involved in the restorative justice movement in Brazil.

We thank the Amazon Restorative Justice Clinic, the Graduate Program in Society Sciences, and the Graduate Program in Nature, Society and Development at the Federal University of Western Pará, and the Graduate Program in Law and Development in the Amazon at the Federal University of Pará, both in Brazil; they are committed to academic discussions and research on environmental issues, providing great impetus for restorative justice initiatives involving Indigenous Peoples and local communities.

We also extend our gratitude to the Court of Justice of Pará, Brazil, where Josineide Pamplona found both motivation and support to carry out judicial work focused on restorative justice for over a decade. Additionally, the court granted her a year and a half of leave to pursue her doctorate in Environmental Sciences, an opportunity that contributed significantly to the development of several ideas presented in this book.

We thank Denise Breton, the executive director of Living Justice Press, for providing its editor Edward Valandra with the necessary time and resources so that he could participate in the cowriting of this book.

We thank Barb Toews for sharing the burden of coproducing this work amid so many challenges: the global South versus North histories, different languages (Portuguese, English, and Lakȟóta), settler and Indigenous worldviews, and so forth. She was, in fact, almost the fifth author of this book.

Finally, we thank the (Grand)Mother Earth for the words we found, and on behalf of her, we thank our mothers, fathers, grandmothers, grandfathers, and all our ancestors. We did our best to defend our beloved relative, the Natural World.

Our gratitude to all!

About the Authors

Waŋblí Wapȟáha Hokšíla (Edward Valandra) is Síčáŋǧu Thitȟuŋwaŋ. He was born and raised in his settler-occupied homeland, the Očhéthi Šakówiŋ Oyáte Makȟóčhe. Until 2016, he was a Professor at Native and non-Native universities and is currently the editor for Living Justice Press (LJP). This small, nonprofit company publishes literature about Indigenous justice, restorative justice, circles, and harms between peoples. His work contributes to comprehending Native understandings of justice and how to apply restorative justice to repairing long-standing and current harms that define settlers' and Indigenous Peoples' relationships. He is the author of numerous articles and books and the editor of the award-winning *Colorizing Restorative Justice: Voicing Our Realities*.

João Salm was born in the Island of Nossa Senhora do Desterro (Florianopolis), Santa Catarina, Brazil, belonging to a settler family that came from Germany and Lebanon. He is an associate professor of restorative justice at Governors State University in Chicago's Southland. João is a Centro Studi Sulla Giustizia Riparativa e La Mediazione member at the University of Insubria, Italy, and a collaborator of the Howard Zehr Institute for Restorative Justice, in the United States. He has worked as a consultant to the United Nations Development Program in Fiji and the Solomon Islands and the United Nations Peacebuilding Fund in Guinea Bissau. He was also a partner with the Canadian Foreign Ministry for the development of restorative justice in Brazil.

Josineide Pamplona is a state judge in Brazil with a doctorate in Environmental Sciences. She comes from a settler family of Spanish origin that dwells in northeastern Brazil, a semiarid region that has historically suffered from prolonged droughts and acute social and economic inequalities. She is currently a member of her country's National Commission for Land Solutions of the National Council of Justice and state coordinator of restorative justice at the Court of Justice of Pará. For about ten years, she led a restorative justice program for children and youth. In addition, she was a member of the Restorative Justice Management Group within the Brazilian judiciary.

Nirson Neto is an anthropologist and associate professor at two public universities in Brazil—Federal University of Pará and Federal University of Western Pará. Some of his ancestors hailed from Portugal and settled in the Amazon region of Brazil. He was born and raised in Pará, a Brazilian state that has suffered the most from the advance of settler colonialism. For more than a decade, he has been developing a restorative justice program for different ethnic groups affected by environmental injustice and harm, such as Indigenous Peoples, quilombolas (a.k.a. maroons in the United States), artisanal fishermen, and Brazil nut gatherers. He has collaborated with the Working Group on Environmental Restorative Justice of the European Forum for Restorative Justice.

Notes

Chapter 1

1. Of course, there are other possible answers. Today, solid scientific evidence shows that the deforestation of rainforests, such as the Amazon, influences the rainfall in other regions. The phenomenon of "flying rivers," large volumes of water vapor that migrate through the air from rainforests to other localities, show the interconnection between different parts of the planet. Large-scale deforestation causes transformations in this natural dynamic, modifying the rainfall regime in rainforests and other places located thousands of miles away.
2. See Edward Valandra's "Living Justice: An Indigenous Perspective." *Exploring Native Justice*, First Nations Development Institute. https://www.firstnations.org/gallery/dr-edward-valandra-wanbli-wap%C8%9Faha-hoksila/.

Chapter 2

1. Antonio Carlos Sant'Ana Diegues. *O mito moderno da natureza intocada*. São Paulo, Hucitec and Nupaub-USP/CEC, 2008.
2. Ashley Dawson et al. *Decolonize Conservation: Global Voices for Indigenous Self-Determination, Land, and a World in Common*. New York and Philadelphia: Common Notions, 2023.
3. Joan Martínez Alier, *The Environmentalism of the Poor: A Study of Ecological Conflicts and Valuation*. Cheltenham, UK: Edward Elgar Publishing, 2003.
4. Dawson et al., p. 31.

5 United Nations, *Transforming Our World: The 2030 Agenda for Sustainable Development.* Available at: https://sdgs.un.org/2030agenda.
6 For more information about the case, see João Salm, Nirson Medeiros da Silva Neto, and Josineide Gadelha Pamplona Medeiros, "Restorative Justice: A Substantive, Ecological, and Intergenerational Approach in the Amazon Region of Brazil." *Contemporary Justice Review: Issues in Criminal, Social, and Restorative Justice* 24, no. 2 (2021).
7 Ailton Krenak. *Ideas to Postpone the End of the World*, translated by Anthony Doyle. Toronto: House of Anansi Press, 2020.
8 Davi Kopenawa and Bruce Albert. *The Falling Sky: Words of a Yanomami Shaman*, translated by Nicholas Elliott and Alison Dundy. Cambridge, MA: Harvard University Press, 2013.

Chapter 3

1 Black Lives Matter. *Climate Justice Is Racial Justice*, available at: https://blacklivesmatter.com/climate-justice-is-racial-justice/.
2 Cited by World Economic Forum, *What Is Environmental Racism and How Can We Fight It?*, 2020. Available at: https://www.weforum.org/stories/2020/07/what-is-environmental-racism-pollution-covid-systemic/#:~:text=It%20was%20African%20American%20civil,toxic%20waste%20facilities%2C%20the%20official.
3 Mary Robinson. *Climate Justice: Hope, Resilience, and the Fight for a Sustainable Future.* New York: Bloomsbury Publishing, 2018.
4 First National People of Color Environmental Leadership Summit. *The Principles of Environmental Justice.* Washington DC, 1991. Available at: https://www.ejnet.org/ej/principles.pdf.

Chapter 4

1 Patty Krawec. *Becoming Kin: An Indigenous Call to Unforgetting the Past and Reimagining the Future.* Minneapolis, Broadleaf Books, 2022.

2. *Good Fire: Indigenous Cultural Burns Renew Life* (https://bioneers.org/good-fire-indigenous-cultural-burns-renew-life-zmbz2108/).
3. Pikyav Field Institute. *Eco-cultural Revitalization.* Available at: http://www.karuk.us/index.php/departments/naturalresources/eco-cultural-revitalization/pikyav-fieldinstitute.
4. *Good Fire: Indigenous Cultural Burns Renew Life*, interview with Bill Tripp.
5. *Good Fire: Indigenous Cultural Burns Renew Life*, interview with Bill Tripp.
6. Tim Ingold. *The Perceptions of the Environment: Essays on Livelihood, Dwelling and Skill.* London and New York: Routledge, 2000.
7. Phillip Descola. *Beyond Nature and Culture*, translated by Janet Lloyd. Chicago: The University of Chicago Press, 2013.
8. Edward Valandra's testimony to South Dakota Board on Geographic Names: the renaming of Harney Peak, 17 April 2015.
9. Descola, *Beyond Nature and Culture.*
10. Ingold, *The Perceptions of the Environment.*
11. Leonardo Boff. *Sustentabilidade: o que é - o que não é.* Petrópolis (RJ, Brazil): Vozes, 2018, p. 46. We translated the excerpt into English.
12. Kay Pranis, Barry Stuart, and Mark Wedge, *Peacemaking Circles: From Crime to Community*, St. Paul, MN: Living Justice Press, 2003, pp. 69–70.
13. Alberto Guerreiro Ramos. *The New Science of Organizations: A Reconceptualization of the Wealth of Nations.* Toronto: University of Toronto Press, 1981.
14. Ben Almassi, *Reparative Environmental Justice in a World of Wounds.* Lanham, MD: Lexington Books, 2021.
15. Alberto Acosta. *O bem viver: uma oportunidade para imaginar outros mundos*, translated by Tadeu Breda. São Paulo: Autonomia Literária and Elefante, 2016, p. 25. We translated the excerpt into English.

Chapter 5

1 Case originally reported in Josineide Gadelha Pamplona Medeiros, Nirson Medeiros da Silva Neto, and Jarsen Luis Guimarães Castro, "Essa é a justiça que queremos": estudo de uma prática restaurativa em contexto de etnogênese indígena no Baixo Tapajós, Amazônia, Brasil," *Contribuciones a las Ciencias Sociales* 6, no. 9 (2023).
2 Elizabeth Elliott. *Security with Care: Restorative Justice and Healthy Societies*. Nova Scotia: Fernwood Publishing, 2011.
3 Kay Pranis. "The Little Book of Circle Processes," in Howard Zehr, Lorraine Stutzman Amstutz, Allan MacRae, and Kay Pranis, *The Big Book of Restorative Justice*. New York: Good Books, 2015.
4 Howard Zehr. "The Little Book of Restorative Justice," in Howard Zehr, Lorraine Stutzman Amstutz, Allan MacRae, and Kay Pranis, *The Big Book of Restorative Justice*. New York: Good Books, 2015.
5 Harold Gatensby. *Message About the History of Circles in Restorative Justice from Harold Gatensby*. Available at: https://www.restorecircles.love/restorative-justice.
6 Pranis, Stuart, and Wedge, *Peacemaking Circles: From Crime to Community*.
7 Carolyn Boyes-Watson. *Peacemaking Circles and Urban Youth: Bringing Justice Home*. St. Paul, MN: Living Justice, 2008.
8 Ella Deloria. *Speaking of Indians* (1944); reprint. Lincoln: University of Nebraska Press, 1998.
9 Deloria. *Speaking of Indians*, p. 17.
10 Deloria. *Speaking of Indians*, p. 20.
11 Deloria. *Speaking of Indians*, p. 20.
12 Deloria. *Speaking of Indians*, p. 25.
13 Robert Yazzie, "Life Comes from It: Navajo Justice Concepts." *New Mexico Law Review* 24, Rev, 175 (1994), 188.
14 Yazzie, "Life Comes from It: Navajo Justice Concepts," footnote 66, 188.
15 The writing of her name as lowercase letters is an option of bell hooks. It is present in several of her

books. In this little book, we decided to use the way the author wrote her name in her works.
16 bell hooks. *All About Love: New Visions*. New York: William Morrow, 2000.
17 Interview with bell hooks, *All About Love*, 19 March 2000, available in: https://www.npr.org/2000/03/19/1071796/all-about-love.

Chapter 6
1 Howard Zehr. "The Little Book of Restorative Justice," p. 19.
2 Howard Zehr. *Changing Lenses: Restorative Justice for Our Times*. Harrisonburg and Kitchener: Herald Press, 2015.
3 Katerina Friesen, managing editor. *Stories of Repair: A Reparative Justice Resource toward Dismantling the Doctrine of Discovery*. Phoenix, AZ: Dismantling the Doctrine of Discovery Coalition, 2021, p. 8.
4 Paulo Freire. *Pedagogy of the Oppressed*, translated by Myra Bergman Ramos. New York and London: Continuum, 2005.